W9-BNP-690

Building a
High Morale
Workplace

Other titles in the Briefcase Books series include:

To learn more about titles in the Briefcase Books series go to
www.briefcasebooks.com

You'll find the tables of contents, downloadable sample chapters, information on the authors, discussion guides for using these books in training programs, and more.

A
Briefcase
Book

Building a
High Morale
Workplace

Anne Bruce

McGraw-Hill

New York   Chicago   San Francisco   Lisbon   London
Madrid   Mexico City   Milan   New Delhi   San Juan
Seoul   Singapore   Sydney   Toronto

The **McGraw·Hill** Companies

3 4 5 6 7 8 9 0   FGR/FGR   0 9 8 7 6 5 4

ISBN 0-07-140618-2

Library of Congress Cataloging-in-Publication Data applied for.

This is a CWL Publishing Enterprises Book, developed and produced for
McGraw-Hill by CWL Publishing Enterprises, John A. Woods, President. For
more information, contact CWL Publishing Enterprises, 3010 Irvington Way,
Madison, WI 53713-3414, www.cwlpub.com.

This publication is designed to provide accurate and authoritative information in regard to the subject matter covered. It is sold with the understanding
that neither the author nor the publisher is engaged in rendering legal,
accounting, or other professional service. If legal advice or other expert
assistance is required, the services of a competent professional person
should be sought.
        —From a Declaration of Principles jointly adopted by a Committee
        of the American Bar Association and a Committee of Publishers

McGraw-Hill books are available at special quantity discounts to use as pre-
miums and sales promotions, or for use in corporate training programs. For
more information, please write to the Director of Special Sales, McGraw-Hill,
2 Penn Plaza, New York, NY 10128. Or contact your local bookstore.

This book is printed on recycled, acid-free paper containing a mini-
mum of 50% recycled de-inked fiber.

Contents

Preface

This is a book about hope—because when there is hope, there is limitless opportunity for managers to create the ultimate high morale workplace, in good times and in bad. This also is a book about how managers inspire employee growth and renewal from day to day, moving workers step by step toward a beacon of light—a light indicating a better tomorrow filled with greater meaning and higher truth.

This book holds very special meaning for me as the author. When my editor, John Woods, called me in New York to see if I was available for this project, I had just returned from Ground Zero, where an hour earlier I stood looking at the still-smoldering wreckage from the terrorist attacks on the World Trade Center.

I have always been driven by my passion for developing the personal best in people, but that's changed. After witnessing the indescribable, I've been filled with an even greater passion. A passion to do something that can in some small way help managers to create and rebuild a high morale work environment while fulfilling my personal quest to help both leaders and their followers rise above the tough times and persevere no matter what. Writing this book is one way of making that quest a reality.

More than ever, managers must try to do everything they can to continually improve and build high employee morale in their organizations. Employees universally need motivation and inspiration. They need something to believe in—a sense of belonging and purpose. They need hope. We all do. I knew that if I could address some of those needs in this book I would be able to give managers a tool that would help guide them to creating a high morale work environment.

Never has there been a time so ripe with opportunity or full of promise for managers to make a significant difference in their organizations and for their people. And never has there been a better time for managers to demonstrate to employees their leadership vitality, creativity, positive energy, and commitment to a healthier and more enjoyable work environment.

Throughout this book, I emphasize that the key to a manager's success is in his or her people. The core feeling that comes from a high morale workplace is simply the reflection of the quality, one-on-one relationships that individual workers have with their managers. It's the trust, respect, and common courtesies that managers show toward their employees on a daily basis that contribute to building exceptional employee performance and to sustaining higher employee morale.

Ralph Waldo Emerson writes in *The Conduct of Life*, "Our chief want in life is somebody who shall make us do what we can." This quote embodies the critical nature and inherent responsibility managers just like you are facing when it comes to developing their people and inspiring employee morale to its highest levels.

Abracadabra—You've Got High Employee Morale

Here's the deal—right up front. There is no such thing as abracadabra when it comes to creating high morale in the workplace. And, with the exception of the mythical pixie dust that exists only at Disney, there is no magic trick or fairy dust to sprinkle on people in hopes of creating a fun, synergistic, and highly productive organization. Achieving those things takes a manager's hard work and dedication. It is my hope that having this book to help you along the way will make that work less difficult.

It is also my desire and hope that you will find this book to be an invaluable resource that you will turn to time and again and that the next time you are called upon to confront one of the many issues of workplace morale, this book will serve as a trusted companion and quick-reference guide when you need it most.

Selecting the Best Ideas for You in This Book

Whether you're reading Chapter 2 on the effects of globalization on employee morale and its connection to how we behave as managers and treat our employees or referencing Chapter 9 on how to win back lost morale when tragedy strikes while learning about the new expectations employees are placing on managers and what to do about it, you'll find gathered within the covers of this book some of the best and most useful ideas on creating a jubilant and uplifting workplace for everyone—from those who have been there, done that.

The ideas in this book come from many talented people. Some are well-known managers and global leaders; others are not so well known, but noticeably effective in their management styles. Some are authors, consultants, scholars, and entrepreneurs. Some are living and some are dead. Maybe you know some of these people and their companies, or perhaps you've read about them and admire their people skills and talent for bringing out the best in others. Regardless of your familiarity with the experts in this book, all of them have proven performance records when it comes to creating extraordinary employee morale and leaving their indelible imprint on the hearts, minds, and souls of those who are fortunate enough to work with them.

And so where do these experts come from? They come from all sectors of the global workplace—business, professions, politics, government, social and non-profit organizations, manufacturing, healthcare, technology, and more. Their countless contributions to this book consist of interviews I have conducted in person and by phone. There are also organizations and people in this book that I have yet to meet in person or interview. Yet, I've studied and researched them and their organizations for years, showcasing their invigorating and morale-boosting management styles in my keynote speeches and workshops I facilitate around the world. When it comes to creating high employee morale, there are lots of people who are doing it right and who love to tell their stories. You'll find those stories and real-world examples in this book.

Purpose of This Book

I wrote this book with a specific purpose in mind. That purpose was not just to have managers read this book and then put it on the shelf to collect dust. I wrote *Building a High Morale Workplace* for managers, like you, to use as a valuable field guide to help shape and increase your chances of success and help ensure the survivability of morale and motivation within your organization.

It was my goal while writing this book that you, the reader, would be able to easily glean important pieces of information and apply them in the most appropriate and effective ways on the job, as quickly as possible.

Manager's Call to Action

Here is where I will make a personal request of you. My request is that you take the wellspring of information in this book—information that will hopefully inform and inspire you—and interpret it as your own personal call to action. In other words, do something with this information. Take these gems of advice and make them come alive where you work. I believe that by doing this you will have the opportunity to create a lasting legacy—the legacy of a valued organization with valued people that survives and thrives over time in a high-spirited, high-energy, high morale workplace.

Special Features

The idea behind the books in the Briefcase Series is to give you practical information written in a friendly, person-to-person style. The chapters are short, deal with tactical issues, and include lots of examples. They also feature numerous boxes designed to give you different types of specific information. Here's a description of the boxes you'll find in this book.

Smart Managing These boxes do just what they say: give you tips and tactics for being smart in promoting employee morale.

 CAUTION! These boxes provide warnings for where things could go wrong when you're dealing with employees.

 Tricks of the Trade These books give you how-to hints for building morale.

 Key Term Every subject has some special jargon and terms. These boxes provide definitions of these concepts.

 For Example It's always useful to have examples of what others have done, either well or not so well. Find these stories in these boxes.

 Tools This identifies boxes where you'll find specific procedures you can follow to take advantage of the book's advice.

 Mistake Proofing How can you make sure you won't make a mistake when managing? You can't, but these boxes will give you practical advice on how to minimize the possibility.

Acknowledgments

If you've ever written a book, you know that it practically takes a village to make it a reality. If you haven't written a book, just take my word for it. I can't say enough about the support and love of family and friends that gets you through when you are sitting at your computer day and night writing for months at a time. From the deepest part of my heart, I'd like to thank all the people who supported me during this project, especially my husband, David, who gives me confidence and guides me back to my purpose with his insight and love; my daughter, Autumn, who inspires me daily with her courageous and uncompromising quest to follow her dreams; my sister, Rose Marie Trammell, the most generous and kind-spirited person I know; and my cousin, Theresa Kautz, whose amazing loyalty and belief in me has never waned. Special appreciation goes to my dear friend Traci Van, for standing by me all these years and for being my inspiration for keeping the faith on a daily basis.

A big thank-you to my editor and friend, John Woods, head of CWL Publishing Enterprises, to whom I'm grateful for calling me that day in New York and inviting me to work with him on this project—he is a person who knows how to keep an author's morale high. Thanks, also, to copyeditor Bob Magnan of CWL for his helpfulness along the way, not to mention that great sense of humor; Nancy Woods, who kept the plates spinning and paid attention to all the details; and McGraw-Hill's Senior Editor, Catherine Dassopoulos, for including me in another Briefcase Book and for always seeing the big picture.

It goes without saying that this book could not have been written without the hundreds of people I interviewed who demonstrate daily their unwavering commitment to creating a more joyful, respectful, humane, esteeming, and spirit-filled place for people to work. This especially includes the firefighters, police officers, medical practitioners, clergy, and people of New York and Washington, D.C. for sharing their heartfelt stories with me.

Finally, I would like to dedicate this book to the victims of September 11, 2001, and to their loved ones.

About the Author

Anne Bruce is the lead author of another popular Briefcase Book, *Motivating Employees* (McGraw-Hill, 1999) and author of the best-selling book, *Leaders—Start to Finish: A Road Map for Developing and Training Leaders at All Levels* (American Society for Training & Development, 2001). She is a popular keynote speaker and inspiring workshop facilitator known for her highly entertaining and engaging presentation style.

A former television talk show host and producer for CBS, Anne has been a featured presenter for The White House, Harvard Law School, Stanford Law School, and the London Institute of Management. Her motivational programs on leadership, customer service, the power of human potential, and an array of communications topics have been featured at worldwide business conferences, by professional associations, and in hundreds of corporations, including Coca-Cola, Sprint, Ben & Jerry's, Southwest Airlines, Southern Company, Lanier Worldwide, Blue Cross/Blue Shield, Paine Webber, Baylor University Medical Center, the American Red Cross, the Conference Board of Europe, and the American Management Association.

For more information on workshops and keynote presentations associated with this book, visit Anne's Web site at www.annebruce.com to get a workshop outline and details on how you can bring this program into your organization. Or you can e-mail questions and comments to anne@annebruce.com. Anne resides in Northern California with her husband David and can be reached by calling 214-507-8242.

Building a High Morale Workplace

Business on Planet Earth, No Longer as We Know It

We have seen the end of business as usual. Simply put, the way we've been running our companies and managing our employees is no more. The atrocities of September 11, 2001 accelerated an unprecedented shift in how we do business and, more importantly, how we manage, care for, and treat the people who work for us.

Business is still about providing great customer service, making a superior product, and producing a healthy return on investment for shareholders. However, to do that and succeed, managers also have to be concerned about their employees and their work environment. They need to know what's involved in creating a high morale workplace where people actually love to go to work, really enjoy their jobs, savor the experiences they have in those jobs, and feel pride, enthusiasm, self-confidence, and a strong motivation to succeed in every project and team effort.

Manager's Challenge

Many managers know the importance of delving into the deeper meaning of their organizations and their work. Business is not just about numbers; it's about people. Managers are realizing, now more than ever, how much it matters for managers to be sensitive to the people who work with them and promote a feeling of community and caring. Today's managers and supervisors have the greatest challenge of their careers before them.

So what is that challenge? I would argue that it's building and boosting and, more specifically, sustaining morale in a workplace that's enveloped by anxieties over change, reorganization, loss of job security, and technology, not to mention the stress and strain of always having to do more with less.

So this is the challenge. It's real and it's here. Are you up for it?

As a leader in your organization, the choices you face are pretty clear. If you want to get the most from your employees (and yourself), you need to make high morale a high priority. It's a competitive necessity.

You need to start creating with your employees the ideal workplace. I like to think of it as the high morale workplace of the 21st century, a workplace that you and your fellow managers and employees, all collaborating, can make happen.

A *high morale workplace* is an environment that engenders excellence and fosters collaboration and a desire to contribute, where employees feel motivated to work hard and smart. Such environments are shaped by intelligent managers who recognize the psychological and business payoffs of high morale.

> **Key Term**
>
> **Morale** How an individual feels about his or her work and the organization. If morale is low, participation is likely to be limited to doing what's required or otherwise expected. Conversely, high morale suggests that individuals will participate with enthusiasm and a sense of commitment.

Co-Creating a High-Performing Workplace

If you and your employees are going to co-create a high morale workplace, then you must have esprit de corps, because morale can exist only when people feel special. American Express has used this strategy quite successfully with its popular slogan, "Membership has its privileges." One of your first steps in co-creating a high morale environment is to establish group identity. Whenever you create a group identity that makes all employees feel good about themselves, you're also creating esprit de corps. So begin by establishing a sense of pride and belonging among the members of your team. Building group morale and building a high morale workplace go hand in hand.

> **Esprit de corps** French term for a sense of unity and common purpose among members of a group. With esprit de corps, people feel special, sharing in something important. What high morale is to individuals, esprit de corps is to the group. They really reinforce one another.

Another way to bring about high morale in an organization is to make sure employees are sufficiently trained, so they can be confident about doing their jobs well. Be sure employees get ongoing opportunities for training and self-directed learning whenever possible, such as recommended reading lists, seminars, group discussions, or brown-bag lunches where employees get together informally and discuss issues and solutions for improvement within the organization or department.

Another way to build morale and promote esprit de corps is through sharing positive experiences and feelings. One thing you can do is initiate a voluntary "good news hour" once a week before work begins, to allow time for employees to share all of the good things that have happened to them on the job in the past week.

Because you're the manager, you significantly and directly influence the level of morale in your organization and department. Pay attention to your employees, show them that you

Home Depot—A Wildly Successful, High-Performing Organization

Five-time recipient of *Fortune* magazine's America's Most Admired Retailer award, Home Depot is considered to be a wildly successful and high-performing organization—a company that's enjoyed year after year of record-breaking profits and has been touted as the largest home improvement company in the nation.

But above all, Home Depot is recognized for its positive corporate culture, a culture that inspires employee commitment and unrelenting morale and enthusiasm. Home Depot operates on the belief that a company that wants to inspire a passionate commitment to taking care of its customers must first show a passionate commitment to taking care of its people. In other words, if you take care of the internal, the external will take care of itself.

The success of Home Depot's positive corporate culture rests on three important points: 1) to treat employees right at all times, 2) to maintain a high morale atmosphere where every employee is an "owner" in the company, not just an employee, and 3) to build a feeling of family, not just among employees but throughout the community. Home Depot shows how it cares about its people with adoption assistance, ethics workshops, a fund that matches dollar-for-dollar employee donations to charities, programs that inspire a diverse workforce, and unpaid leave for up to six months for employees with serious family problems.

Home Depot's credo: live the passion and success follows.

care about them, listen to what they have to say, and discover how quickly you'll be able to create an atmosphere that's capable of surviving continuous change, stress, and fear of the unknown. Start now and watch your environment become wildly successful.

What Are You Doing to Build Morale?

The impact of morale is wide and varied. Morale directly affects the motivation of employees and can greatly influence their ability to perform. The attitude of your employees toward you and the organization can make all the difference. Answer these questions to see if you and your organization are demonstrating the key characteristics and behaviors necessary to build morale:

- Are managers rewarding workers for exceeding the expectations of their jobs? Remember the famous words of Dallas cosmetics mogul, the late Mary Kay Ash: "The two things that people want more than sex or money are recognition and praise." What have you done lately for employees who contribute regularly to product and service improvements or help reduce the costs of operation without sacrificing quality?

* Are you really empowering your people? Or are you just giving them responsibility and then telling them how to do the job? How often do you grant workers more responsibility for achieving greater performance and productivity in their jobs? Are you giving them the authority to use company assets to quickly satisfy customer needs?

- What do you do so employees feel safe about expressing their differences without fear of management reprisal? Do you review and seriously consider their grievances on a timely basis? To maintain high morale, deal with differences as quickly as possible. The faster you settle a grievance, the lower the levels of disruption and the higher the levels of morale and employee satisfaction.

It's been proven over and over again that the environment

Putting on the Ritz for Greater Morale

How can a company empower its employees? Take a look at the Ritz-Carlton hotels—twice the recipient of the prestigious Malcolm Baldrige National Quality Award. Ritz Carlton authorizes its employees to spend up to $2,000 to fix any customer's problem—right on the spot, with no questions asked. We're not just talking about managers or supervisors here. We're talking about every single Ritz Carlton employee, from bellhop to front desk clerk, from housekeeper to gift shop worker. The Ritz Carlton has successfully created an exemplary model for trusting employees and empowering them to do the right thing, which is also a great way to build their self-esteem and morale.

must be right for morale to flourish. There are no set rules or particular management styles that will transform your environment. Just know that you can't do it alone.

Discuss with your employees ways to co-create the ideal environment, a place where you all will feel great about working together. Then take it upon yourself to experiment, try out new ideas, and build on the successes of your team. Encourage your employees to do the same.

Each of the following morale boosters relates to a particular management style that any caring and spirited manager or supervisor can put into action for his or her employees.

Five Steps to Create High-Spirited Morale Boosters

There are five steps you can take to create high-spirited morale boosters. Let's review those now.

Step 1. Become a Genuine and Authentic Manager

Smart Managing

Authentic Genuine and honest in dealing with other people, yet also considerate of their feelings. Employees know where an authentic manager stands on any issue that arises. Employees respect an authentic manager and know they have his or her respect as well.

Authentic managers care a great deal about their people and make them feel special and valued. Their compliments are real and from the heart, not phony and manipulative. Authentic leaders sustain morale by taking the time to listen to their workers, to understand their emotional needs, and to support those needs by asking questions and demonstrating genuine concern.

Step 2. Tune into the Emotional Needs of Your Employees

It's critical that you have a basic understanding of the emotional needs of your workers:

- Praise and recognition
- Achievement and advancement
- Sense of belonging

- Pride and confidence
- Challenge and excitement
- Love and support

Try using this emotional needs checklist as a way of staying in tune with employees and making sure that their inner most needs and desires are being met. In addition, you can use this list to match jobs and assignments with individuals according to their strongest emotional need. By doing so, you can expect greater enthusiasm and commitment. In other words, this is a guaranteed morale booster!

Questions to Sustain Morale

How do managers start down the road to sustain morale? They ask questions like these:

- What matters most to you about the outcome of this situation?
- How are you feeling about this?
- Help me understand. Can you tell me more?"
- What concerns you most?"
- How would you handle this?"

Step 3. Generate a Spirit of Gratitude

It's all summed up in two little words: thank you! If you want to be a manager who creates high morale, then instill the spirit of gratitude on a daily basis and set the example. A pat on the back, a short thank-you note, an e-mail of appreciation, or a jubilant voice mail from you can do wonders to charge up an employee. As a leader in your organization, it's your responsibility to spread the spirit of gratitude. When you do, watch the level of motivation, morale, and pride rise significantly.

Here's a suggestion. Ask for volunteers with a

What Do They Need?   Smart Managing

Ask your employees to review the list of emotional needs and select the areas most important to satisfying those needs. Then discuss with each employee ways in which they can tie their specific needs to the specific tasks and functions required of them on the job. When your employees are meeting their emotional needs and those needs are in alignment with their talents and job responsibilities, you have an unbeatable formula for success!

Say Thank You
At Lands' End they've created small cards with special meanings to thank one another internally and to boost daily morale. It's an easy way to encourage employees and managers to express their appreciation.

passion for the positive and then start your own "gratitude team" or "just because committee." Have the teams come up with ways to encourage daily affirmations throughout the organization. It's a great way to involve employees in building morale.

Step 4. Spread Contagious Enthusiasm Wherever You Go

Keeping Their Respect
You're the manager. You set the tone. Never ask employees to do anything you wouldn't do yourself. Be enthusiastic. Show employees by your example that if you act enthusiastic, you will be enthusiastic! And remember: your behavior is the role model for your employees—for better or worse.

If it's high performance that you want, then it's important that you, too, maintain high performance goals and contagious enthusiasm for your work. Remember that high morale starts with you, so be careful to practice what you preach if you are to maintain credibility among your workers. Then spread the word about how important everyone's job is to the overall success of the company and provide workers with examples about how much they are valued.

Step 5. Treat Employees as Humans, Not Just Workers

Boost morale by acknowledging the human side of doing business and nurturing an atmosphere of high self-esteem by treating people like ... people. Humanness and humanity are the cornerstones of self-esteem and high morale. Start by creating a "whole-person database." Show that you appreciate your employees and that you're interested in what interests them.

Take time to ask them about their hobbies, musical instruments they play, foreign countries they've visited, and so on. Who's a professional singer? Who's a gourmet chef? Who's an equestrian? Enjoy your employees. Help them to be humans, not just workers.

> ### Go Beyond Job Descriptions
> **Smart Managing**
>
> Don't let your employees get stuck on job descriptions. Instead, point out the value and importance of each individual's job. Also, recognize what each can contribute: it's a good way to build morale and esprit de corps as well as to discover skills and talents that may not show in the usual tasks and assignments.

These are just some of the many ways you as a manager can work with your employees to create spirited morale boosters. Remember: employees need and want managers who can empathize with their needs and who genuinely try to co-create with them an environment in which everyone feels valued and respected, no matter what's going on around them or what changes they may be facing.

> ### Whole-Person Database
> **TOOLS**
>
> Collect information from willing employees about themselves. What are their special talents? Their interests? Their exceptional accomplishments? Their favorite movies, songs, sports, and hobbies? Who's a pilot? Who collects porcelain dolls? Who's a stand-up comedian? Such information becomes a fantastic way to network internally and build ongoing morale and pride.
>
> Appoint a team to acquire and build on the information as a networking tool and valuable company resource. Who knows what could develop? Maybe some employees will form after-work pottery or cooking classes, support groups, travel clubs, skydiving teams, or maybe even a company choir or band! As you build your whole-person database, you'll discover untapped and invaluable resources within your department. And, best of all, your employees will feel that you value and care for them as whole persons, not just employees.

Make Your Company More of a Community, Less of a Corporation

Thirty years ago, if you'd asked the typical manager in an organization for a definition of morale in the workplace, the answer may have been something like "Morale is a commitment to the company's objectives, controlling bottom-line expenses, and annihilating the competition." Pose that same question to a manager today and you'll likely get answers like the following:

- "Morale is the lifeblood of our organization and gives us meaningful purpose."
- "The level of morale in our organization tells us how successful we really are."
- "Morale is an attitude. It represents our determination and fortitude."
- "Our company's morale tells the world who we are and what we are all about—people!"

Obviously, different decades have different ideas about morale in the workplace. And, as the famous author and poet Maya Angelou says, "When you know better, you do better." In other words, managers today can no longer hide behind the excuse, "We just didn't know any better," because we certainly do know better.

We know that if high morale in the workplace is to survive and thrive and if managers are going to focus on creating a better future for their employees and their organizations, then it's time that managers at all levels concern themselves with nurturing a stronger sense of community within the organization. Morale partly involves the feeling of community that you build as a manager. It means taking your organization's culture to the next level and bringing lots of positive energy to the workplace.

Cultivating Community

There are several keys to cultivating community within an organization:

- **Be a manager who promotes the organization's culture, values, and mission.** Model and encourage loyalty and fierce commitment to a better workplace for all.
- **Hire the people who are the right fit with your organization's community and culture.** Try using Nordstrom's rule of thumb for hiring: Hire for attitude and train for skill.
- **Coach and mentor people to their highest potential.** Recognize and reward results with fanfare and facilitate each and every employee's success and career growth whenever possible.
- **Integrate new hires so that they feel welcome.** Eliminate the corporate generation gap by doing away with employee numbers that correspond with dates of hire. Make new employees feel like they've been part of the community in your organization since the beginning.
- **Be an organization everyone wants to work for.** Build a community reputation that goes beyond culture and tradition. Exclaim to the world that your organization is the

> ### A Feeling of Belonging TRICKS OF THE TRADE
>
> Managers working in high morale firms are using an effective technique to create a community feeling for new employees. They don't play by the numbers.
>
> Too many companies assign their employees numbers that correspond to their dates of hire, thereby turning numbers into badges of pride and dividing employees. But managers seeking to create a feeling of belonging among employees can easily avoid falling into this corporate generation gap by not telling employees their hiring numbers.

"employer of choice," both internally and externally. Tell the world that this is a place where people are valued, treated with respect, and honored for their differences. Southwest Airlines has been doing this with great success for more than 30 years. The result? There's never a shortage of applicants or hopeful new hires beating down their door.

The Intangible Proof of Morale: Can You Feel It?

When you come in contact with an organization where morale is high, you can sense it immediately. Here are some of the characteristics of such organizations:

- esprit de corps
- positive attitude
- cheerfulness
- confidence
- generosity
- hope
- high self-esteem
- determination
- meaningful purpose
- mutual support
- loyalty

It All Adds Up to the Intangible

It's no secret that businesses with exceptional morale have a very real competitive edge. It's not just about having a superior product or service, or about fancy offices in a high-rise building, or about lower prices than the competition. It's not even related to material things. It's about the intangible, the feelings that are transmitted from one employee to another and then on to the customer—feelings like esprit de corps, a can-do state of mind, and a positive attitude. Morale is about creating an environment that conveys these feelings. As this transformation takes place, you will feel that your organization is behaving less like a corporation and more like a community.

Rally to a Higher Purpose

As a manager, it's your job to foster a sense of community and teamwork any way you can. Keep in mind that today many people are looking for ways to rally around a larger purpose—a purpose that goes beyond the corporate mantra and the bottom line. Acknowledge this need for a higher purpose by helping to create a true feeling of community among your employees. Let that feeling start within the organization and then grow outward. Here are a few ways to do this:

- Employees participating in relief efforts
- Donating holiday party funds to charitable causes
- Building a playground for disadvantage kids, like Ben &

Jerry's franchise operators did in Key West, Florida during one of their annual retreats.

Creating a sense of internal and external community will build morale and bring people together. As a manager, it's your responsibility to be a key player in that effort.

How Best-Run Companies Keep Their People Pumped Up

Are you looking for examples of how to fire up your people—regardless of the work they do or where they do it? Here are a few classic morale-boosting examples of what some companies and their leaders are doing or have done to set a different pace and build communities bursting with morale and hope.

Case Study: Kryptonite—Tough on Crime, Gentle on People

Some people might consider working at a company that makes locks for bicycles, recreational gear, and laptops kind of boring. Not here. And not under the leadership of Gary Furst, CEO of Kryptonite, a Boston-area firm.

According to Furst, if your only way of trying to boost morale is with money, then you can forget it. There's always going to be another company out there with a bigger carrot to dangle. So Kryptonite execs take a more creative approach to keeping morale high and pumping up their people on a regular basis.

The leaders meet a couple of times a month outside of their offices to come up with ways to keep employees motivated and committed to attaining company goals. One of their favorite strategies includes wearing costumes. Once, for example, Furst dressed in a kilt and face paint like Scotsman William Wallace from the Oscar-winning movie *Braveheart* and, accompanied by a bagpiper, he passed out bonus checks to his employees.

Kryptonite boasts it is a different kind of place to work and here are some examples of what sets this company apart:

- The edgy lock-maker describes its people this way: "Passionate, fanatical, driven, consumed. Perhaps we're the one's who should be locked up." How's that for company morale?

- To celebrate five years of no lost time due to accidents, the company held a steak and lobster feast for its employees.
- Furst and other company leaders have dressed up as women, dyed their hair green, and hired magicians, musicians, and comedians to entertain their employees at company events and various other activities.
- Kryptonite kids get to attend holiday parties and Easter egg hunts.
- Instead of holding the typical company picnic, the firm creates teams that lead fierce but fun competitive events and games for all ages.
- Barbecues are held every other Friday during the summer months.

Furst believes that managers have to find innovative, provocative, fun ways to boost employee morale and motivation. He stands firm on his belief: "Work can either be a drag or a lot of fun." It's clear that working at Kryptonite is no drag!

Senior Managers Wash Employees' Cars

While employees of lock-maker Kryptonite were celebrating a record month of business with a barbecue and ice cream, the senior management team washed everyone's cars. According to CEO Gary Furst, managers have to do stuff that's not expected and constantly keep people guessing. It's got to be interesting!

Case Study: Land O' Lakes—Leader in Making People Feel Special

"Building on our best" has long been the tradition at Land O' Lakes, a long-time leader and innovator of dairy foods and agricultural services headquartered in Arden Hills, Minnesota. So when Dan Hanson was named president of the Fluid-Dairy Division, he quickly became frustrated with what seemed to be going on. As Hanson put it, "People didn't seem to be finding meaning in work, they didn't seem to be shining, and there was an energy missing."

So Hanson took on something of a personal crusade for developing the essence of caring and community in the work-place. Hanson had battled cancer and that experience became the catalyst for building a more caring and people-oriented work environment for his employees. "It gave me a sense of urgency," says Hanson. "I knew I had to rediscover the meaning of my work." Hanson took his philosophies even further and wrote two books on the subject: *A Place to Shine: Emerging from the Shadows at Work* (Butterworth-Heinemann, 1996), and *Cultivating Common Ground: Releasing the Power of Relationships at Work* (Butterworth-Heinemann, 1997).

Hanson knows that when employees don't find meaningful purpose or meaningful relationships in their work, it's not their fault. The problem isn't with the people, he contends. It's with an oppressive work environment that stifles morale and creativity. Hanson says that managers who want to foster internal communities must restructure their organizations and change how employees interrelate. His philosophy: "Feeling connected to your work brings energy to the workplace."

Hanson then initiated this four-step action plan to prop up morale and turn things around in his division:

1. **Find out why people feel alienated.** Hanson decided to address both the organizational and the personal work-place problems. His belief is that the organization cannot grow in a positive and healthy direction unless it first treats its employees like people.

2. **Identify pockets of wellness and cultivate a feeling of community among employees.** To foster the feeling of internal community at Land O'Lakes, Hanson identified what he calls "pockets of wellness." In other words, even if the organization's system is sick and dysfunctional to some degree, there are always people within the system who are doing things right, employees who feel connected to their work and create positive energy and high morale. Uncovering

these pockets is essential, according to Hanson.

3. **Understand that community starts at the grassroots, not at the top.** Hanson says that people feel much better about themselves when the organization succeeds because of them and not because management deemed that the company was going to roll out some program that employees would execute to management's liking. For example, when Grand Forks, North Dakota, was flooded in 1997, the Land O' Lakes team in that city pulled together to control the damage. That experience became the model for the kind of exceptional action a community-oriented team can make possible.

4. **Tell your employees when they've succeeded.** Hanson says you have to tell your employees when they've made major strides and accomplishments, because people want to feel appreciated, to feel special.

Since making his mark at Land O' Lakes and publishing his successful management philosophies, Hanson accepted an early retirement from the firm and is now a full-time professor of communications at Augsburg College in Minneapolis, where he continues to share with his students his vision of happiness and fulfillment in the workplace.

TRICKS OF THE TRADE

Creating More Meaning

Professor Dan Hanson, former president of Land O' Lakes Fluid-Dairy Division, suggests that managers start by discussing the undiscussable with their employees. Ask employees what's getting in the way of relationships. Clear out all assumptions. Get to the heart of the matter and find out which processes are working and which ones aren't. His personal philosophy: "Feeling connected to your work brings energy to the workplace."

Case Study: Craigslist—Boosting the Morale of an Entire City

If you're in the San Francisco Bay area, just ask around and you'll find someone who's participated in Craigslist (www.craigslist.com). It's the plugged-in place to be if you're looking for a roommate, a dog walker, a career makeover, software, a new car, or a travel companion.

In today's cyberspace world, we seem to be losing contact with our neighbors. Heck, we don't even know who our neighbors are any more. Yet, we crave contact with them. It's the same thing in most companies today. Throughout virtual workplaces everywhere, employees crave contact with fellow workers and their managers. That's the human condition.

And that's where Craigslist comes in. Founder and CEO Craig Newmark knows about community and he also knows how to bolster pride, enthusiasm, and excitement among millions of people with his virtual community bulletin board for the Bay Area. A day doesn't go by when an online visitor isn't screaming, "Hey, why isn't there a craigslist in my city?!"

So now you're thinking, "You've got to be kidding. I'm having a hard enough time creating high morale in my own organization, let alone try to boost the good feelings of an entire city of online followers. How does he do it?"

Newmark says that his intent is inclusive, to humanize and democratize the Internet. He created Craigslist to give people a voice and a sense of belonging. That's what creates high morale among community members and that's what creates high morale among your employees.

The right kind of forum connects people to each other, building a community. That forum doesn't have to be on the Internet, of course: that's just a medium.

Newmark suggests considering the structure of a large organization—corporate, government, or other. Over time, people on the frontline start to feel stifled and unappreciated because they don't feel like anyone is listening to them or they have a voice. That's when morale takes a dive and people give up trying. To counteract this tendency, a manager can take steps to ensure that employees have a voice.

That's what Newmark has done with Craigslist. Every person can be heard in a particular forum. The Craigslist community is about people helping one another and caring about one

Whole Human Beings

It's easy for a manager to focus on the work and neglect the workers, especially as we're all trying to do more with less—and faster. But when we do, we miss something vital.

Craig Newmark once commented about the people in his Craigslist community: "These people are like me; they spend a lot of time on their computers and rarely get to know the neighbors. Deep down inside of us, we have a need to know people around us, to connect." What about your employees? Do they focus on their jobs and their separate responsibilities to the detriment of their sense of community and their connections with others?

another. In that sense, it's just like any other organization, except that it's in cyberspace rather than bricks and mortar.

Fans seek out Newmark to tell him how Craigslist has transformed their lives by helping them connect: a musician's got a gig that jump-started his career, an adopted son was reunited with his birth mother, a roommate became a spouse. Newmark is a hero to hundreds and hundreds of strangers, because he created a community where people can connect.

What Newmark did for strangers with his Web site you can do for your employees with the resources at your disposal. Just take a few moments and think about the ways in which you can help your employees build a sense of community.

A Better Workplace Starts Here, Right Now, with You

The beginning of this chapter revealed the great changes that each one of us is facing as managers. But that is an understatement. Not only is business "not as usual" anymore, but we as managers are "not as usual" anymore either. Corporate largesse must be backed by every manager's personal commitment to developing the excellence and potential within each and every employee, an undeniable spirit of caring, love and trust in the people, contagious enthusiasm and real excitement, and a genuine belief in a better tomorrow. This is what creating a high morale workplace is all about. Let this first chapter mark the start of a new beginning for you as a manager and your quest to create a high-performing, high morale workplace.

Manager's Checklist for Chapter 1

❑ Create esprit de corps among your employees, because morale can be high only when people feel special.

❑ Pay attention to your employees. Show them that you care about them. Listen to what they have to say—and then take action.

❑ Reward workers for exceeding the expectations of their jobs. Acknowledge employees who contribute regularly to product and service improvements or help reduce the costs of operation without sacrificing quality.

❑ To keep morale high, review employee grievances promptly and settle them quickly.

❑ Tune into the emotional needs of your employees and match those needs to their jobs.

❑ Generate the spirit of gratitude and spread enthusiasm.

❑ Nurture an atmosphere of high self-esteem. Treat people like whole persons. Start a whole-person database.

❑ Make your company more of a community, less of a corporation.

❑ Create a feeling of belonging for new hires. Eliminate employee numbers that correspond with dates of hire.

The Effects of Globalization on Morale

Maybe you'd like to have fresh sea bass for dinner. No problem. There's probably a restaurant or seafood market nearby that gets shipments daily from Chile. And do you really know where your clothes, car, laptop computer, and color copier were made? Do you care? The fact is, that management report you're working on from your office in Cleveland, which you just printed on Canadian paper, with ink from who knows what country, using your laptop, which was probably made in Mexico or Taiwan, is proof that globalization is upon us—you and me—and its effect on how managers maintain and sustain high employee morale is engulfing companies big and small.

Globalization has become ingrained in our assumptions about how we do business, as well as how we behave as managers and the way we treat our employees, both near and far. A one-minute telephone call to Barcelona from the U.S. is less than a dime and the popularity of entertainers, like Britney Spears and Brad Pitt, has taken the entertainment industry's image of American celebrity status and propelled it to a global phenomena.

There's a lot to take in when it comes to keeping up with this global society of ours. In a flash the Internet brings us an overwhelming supply of news, shopping, and music—and an unlimited array of information. A manager's readiness to handle the onslaught of what global-

> **Globalization** A process by which businesses, companies, and social institutions operate internationally and work methods and policies are adopted on a global scale.
>
> **Globalism** Belief that political policies should take worldwide issues into account before focusing on national or state concerns and their advocacy.

ization delivers and its impact on workers is critical to how he or she will fare in the new millennium. The further a manager has to reach to succeed globally in business, the further he or she will have to reach in order to stay in close touch with employees and remain connected to them so that management's presence will be felt.

But I'm Too Small to Be Global!

If you're thinking, "I'm too small to be global," think again. Global reach is all around us and size doesn't matter. Even Jane Doe, the one-woman business consultancy firm operating out of the corner of her bedroom with rollers in her hair and wearing pink fuzzy slippers, can today just as easily be a powerful and effective global player from her loft in SoHo, her farm in Vermont, or her houseboat in Sausalito. If your business can function using a computer and a telephone line, then you're globally capable.

The transformation of our shrinking world is putting the pressure on some managers, even ones in the smallest of companies or mom-and-pop shops. Businesses and their managers will soon be expected to act both global and local in their operations and in the treatment of customers and employees, no matter what size they are or where they're domiciled.

It's a Small, Small World

Globalization signals that the world is getting smaller. And that message has hit home with a vengeance. As Tom Peters points out in his book, *The Circle of Innovation* (New York: Knopf, 1997), "You've heard of 'global village.' I say a village is too big. Try 'global block.' Better yet, try 'global mall.'" What Peters is saying is that not one single manager is more than a fraction of a second away from any other business person or employee, anywhere in the world. When you stop to think about that and the residual affects, it's really quite astounding and life-changing—both personally and professionally.

Need a computer consultant? You can hire one as easily in Bangalore, India as you can in Silicon Valley. Need a business partner and financial backer for your doggie treats company in Jacksonville, Florida? You may find the perfect match in Louisville, Kentucky or somewhere in the United Kingdom. And then there's the growing popularity and empowering effects of distance learning, sometimes called e-learning—an innovative approach to traditional classroom training, where employees can live and work in Omaha and attend online classes at Harvard without moving to Cambridge to do so.

> **Key Term**
>
> **Distance learning/e-learning** A general term for systems that connect learners with distributed learning resources and integrated combinations of technologies designed to support interactive learning among people who are not physically present in the same location. Using audioconferencing, videoconferencing, online streaming video presentations, and analogs, distance learning can reach globally to train unlimited numbers of people in a never-ending list of subjects.

Be Fanatical About Fanatically Excited People!

There is no greater or more powerful weapon for an organization than an army of fanatically excited and engaged people! Does "fanatical" sound too strong? It's not. Fanaticism implies extreme enthusiasm, which is exactly what managers should be aiming for when it comes to creating a high morale workplace in today's challenging, globalized society.

Are you fanatical about creating high employee morale? You should be.

But it takes something more. It takes employee rejuvenation on a global scale.

Fanaticism

"Fanatical" is defined as excessively enthusiastic about a particular belief, cause, or activity. In some contexts, it has some definitely negative associations. Yet is being extreme in the efforts required to create something extraordinary and filled with passion something bad? Not at all! It's managing smart to be wildly enthusiastic and committed to a specific end result.

Smart Managing

Global Rejuvenation

Managers must get creative if they are to fire up and invigorate the vitality of their employees who are spread far and wide across the map. Managers who work at renewing the energy of their employees on a global scale are looking to the future and what's going to be required in tomorrow's high morale work environment.

Here are some ways to creating a rejuvenated global feeling for your employees:

- *Connect workers to a bigger purpose.* No matter how far away they may be, help your employees see the big picture of their efforts. Connect people to a greater purpose by explaining regularly the value of what they contribute to the entire organization's winning strategy. That will help give them context for thinking more strategically about their individual jobs—even for employees in the most remote areas of the world.
- *Infuse enthusiasm in distant locations of your company.* You don't have to be on site to infuse enthusiasm and an upbeat attitude in your global workers. Communicate frequently. Give people lots of information so that they con-

tinue to feel motivated about all the new projects going on at the home office. Tell them how they can duplicate successful programs in their locations—and be specific. Encourage celebrations and ask for feedback on what turns people on in different locales.

- *Laugh out loud online.* Humor is appreciated in every culture. Just be sensitive to the culture you're addressing and to what you say and how you say it. Share your humorous stories with everyone and get employees to laugh out loud online. Take time to translate for people what a specific humorous event may look like in their culture, then offer a similar explanation as to why or how something may be funny in your neck of the woods. Nothing brings people together faster than shared humor.
- *Encourage global innovation.* The mantra is "Innovate or abdicate." That holds true no matter where you live and work. When your organization is global, innovative thinking is a standard requirement. Get the wheels turning in employees' heads worldwide. Ask them to create their own customized innovation program. Offer resources like books or online courses for creative thinking and stimulating inspirational ideas. Make innovation the theme of your next audioconferencing or videoconferencing meeting.
- *Conquer complacency when you sense it.* Complacency kills employee morale. A global operation and its people simply cannot thrive and remain motivated when complacency creeps in. Oliver Wendell Holmes, Sr. wrote in *The Autocrat of the Breakfast Table*: "I find the great thing in this world is not so much where we stand, as in what direction we are moving." As a manager, you must keep people moving forward and continue to fight against illusions of security in employees' past successes. Pump people up with visions of what's to come and what can be. The message worldwide is clear: innovate or abdicate.

High Morale = Synergy and Growth:
The Ogilvy Story

Decades ago, one of the world's most powerful and creative geniuses in advertising history, the late David Ogilvy, was lamenting the fact that his successful ad agency had exploded in growth to include 350 employees. His first reaction was that this was going to become a big headache and an unmanageable problem. But then the great value and significance of the agency's high-employee morale kicked in and shed positive light on the possibilities of going global.

Ogilvy's Synergistic "Aha" Moment

David Ogilvy experienced an "aha" moment when he soon realized that if 350 of his employees were genuinely excited, engaged, and enthusiastic to work at the famous agency and if each of them had just 10 friends that they would brag to about their jobs, then there would be 3,500 enthusiastic and excited people out there walking the streets of New York City spreading fanatically positive and exciting stories and messages about the firm. And imagine if those 3,500 people all went to business meetings, charity events, parties, and grand openings and started talking up how great it was to work at Ogilvy, this would create even more synergy by word-of-mouth and continue to boost employee morale even higher. And it did.

The legendary advertising guru was practicing globalization before globalization was a buzzword and before there was an Internet to make it so much easier to achieve this reality.

Here, set deeply in the roots of the Ogilvy culture, was the evolution of one man's thoughts, talents, work ethic, and unlimited enthusiasm, all spread worldwide and translated into much more than a defining business strategy. Ogilvy's synergistic approach became a destiny that gave employees purpose, meaning, and pride. It also created a highly productive, high morale workplace. Today Ogilvy (a member of the WPP Group) appropriately calls itself, "The most local of the internationals, the most international of the locals," and services more Fortune Global 500 companies than any other agency in the world.

Internet Synergy Revs up Employee Morale Worldwide

Just think how much more powerful your influence can be in today's global workforce than it ever was for David Ogilvy way back then—he had word of mouth, but you've got the Internet at your fingertips. That means with the Web you can multiply that same networking technique that Ogilvy used—but the magnitude of your reach and the huge numbers of people that you can influence is mind-boggling. With the power of the Internet, your message and enthusiasm for employee morale can spread worldwide. That means your ability to create a high-spirited, unbeatable high morale global workplace is now a reality.

Think Globally, Act Locally

You're probably thinking, "Surely it can't all be that easy." Well, nothing worthwhile is ever easy, so here's the catch. In this global society, managers must be prepared to effectively lead by responding to the needs of their local markets, while respecting and honoring the uniqueness of worldwide cultures and their differences.

In the early 1960s, Sony CEO Akio Morita taught his people this still popular and appropriate mantra: "Think globally, act locally." The point he was making was that certain management practices, like treating people with respect and dignity, are universal, as are establishing codes of conduct and work principles or practicing core values. These are all things that transcend geographical boundaries. At the same time, managers should never lose sight of the fact that employees of different cultures, in different countries, must be respected and appreciated individually as well and not lumped together with how we do things in our own small corner of the world. When we don't respect the differences of people from other cultures, we chip away at employee morale and instill a feeling of distance and indifference, rather than unity and global strength.

> ### Disney's Global Reality Check
>
> Upon the opening of Disneyland Paris, Disney learned a few difficult lessons about employee preferences in a very different culture from their Anaheim and Orlando operations. For example, managers in France do not tell their employees how long they can wear their hair or what constitutes "proper grooming," which the Disney corporation strictly enforces among all of its U.S. employees. And unlike no-drinking-on-the-job rules at American amusement parks, Disney quickly discovered that the French do indeed like to have a glass of wine with their lunch.

High Morale Is High Morale, Anywhere You Go in the World

No matter where you go in the world, high morale is high morale. It is a deep human need and desire for employees to feel good about themselves and demonstrate positive attitudes about what they are contributing to the organization, a need and desire that can be felt universally when managers of every nationality help create a working environment that encourages people to be happy, productive, and high-spirited.

IKEA Creates a High Morale Culture

If you want to see a great example of global efficiency and high-employee morale in an international workplace, then take a close look at IKEA. The innovative Swedish furniture company, known worldwide for combining good furniture design with great function and affordable pricing, is easily recognized by its blue and yellow logo—also the colors of the Swedish flag and source of employee pride at IKEA international headquarters, in Helsingborg, Sweden.

Here's an organization where global management gets the full admiration and respect of its employees. Even with more than 150 stores in at least 29 countries, IKEA manages to keep important corporate values and philosophies globally consistent, along with its commitment to preserving the environment—all of which are employee pride builders and morale boosters no matter what languages you speak.

Commitment to the Environment

IKEA employees worldwide, some 44,000 of them, play a key role in the environment and effecting positive change. Each IKEA store has an environmental training coordinator for store co-workers. The objective of the training is to give people insight into and an understanding of the environment and how to preserve it. More than a decade ago IKEA adopted a systematic approach to environmental issues and through the years employees have achieved a variety of environmental accomplishments, from IKEA's use of improved products and materials to preserving Europe's precious ancient forests. All, according to the company, have been "successes which have made us proud and filled us with enthusiasm."

Other IKEA global morale builders include:

- A code of ethics for its suppliers worldwide that focuses on positive working conditions for everyone and protecting the environment.
- Coordinating programs in Northern India to make education more readily available for women and children.
- Teaming with UNICEF to fight child labor worldwide.

It's the Death of Distance and the Birth of Unlimited Opportunity

For managers who are leading and influencing a global workforce with whom they are trying to build relationships and ongoing high morale, here's the challenge: *working together, apart.*

Yep, you read it right. Managers are now faced with creating a team feeling even though team members may be spread as far apart as Kalamazoo and Timbuktu. And even if your workforce isn't quite global at this point, you may still have employees telecommuting between downtown Detroit and the 'burbs. It remains a special challenge if you're not interacting on a daily basis with your people, face to face, no matter how close or far apart those people might be.

The Future Is Here and So Are Virtual Teams

With the imminent death of distance, there is a great rebirth of opportunity taking place. It's called *virtuality*, the inherent ability or potential to bring people together as one team, working on the same projects, in unison, even though they may reside on different continents.

> **Virtuality** Reality that is not defined by concrete parameters, the power of acting without a physical presence. In our context, it's the inherent ability or potential to bring people together as one team, working on the same projects, in unison, even though they may reside on different continents.

As a manager, you'll have to try out your own techniques for making your presence felt among the people you lead across the planet. And that can be tricky. However, the future is here and virtual teams are on the rise; learning to manage them so that morale stays high and employee confidence in your leadership remains steady will be the toughest part.

Managers Know What Matters

But here's the good news—it can be done! The key is keeping track of people and how they're doing. Know what matters to you and know what matters to your people,

> **Virtual teams** Virtual teams consist of people who may never see or meet one another. They may never see or meet their manager either. Employees who make up virtual teams may rarely speak to their managers and yet, they can function as an effective and synchronistic group. They do this by working primarily in cyberspace.

regardless of where they live. Learn to use the newest technologies that will keep you close, like cyberspace auditoriums and virtual conference rooms.

Get Input from Suzie in Switzerland, Not Just Dan down the Hall

It's so easy to simply ask for input from those closest in proximity to you. And why not? It's faster and more convenient. Plus, you know Bob and like his ideas. But in this global workplace, it's important that everyone be included, no matter how far away.

Don't succumb to old habits. You're a global manager, managing a global village, so act like one. It all comes down to perspective and how you treat people. If you treat people like they are 10,000 miles away, they will feel 10,000 miles away. But if you treat people like they are within a moment's reach, then they will feel that way too.

One effective management technique to include people is to ask your employees to come up with a list of all the benefits of working in a virtual environment. This will give you fast insight into the strengths the team perceives in this new workplace reality and which teams are making the most of it all. Next, ask workers to share with you a list of the special challenges that they confront by being part of a long-distance team. So, for example, if a number of team members say that getting together once a month would be helpful to them, then look into the availability of a virtual meeting room where hundreds of workers from all corners of the globe can meet each month without leaving their desks.

By taking time to evaluate the pros and cons of a virtual workplace, you can begin to clarify the challenges and develop your strengths for leading and motivating people from afar.

Meet Me in Cyberspace

If you're a manager in a large organization, you may already be leading teams and building employee morale in cyberspace. Many networked teams in big companies are doing this by way of their organization's local area network (LAN). But there's also an easier way to manage cyber teams and the size of your organization doesn't matter. Managers are now bypassing the LAN and working directly on the Internet with their employees. After all, the Internet is the biggest and best network available, so why not use it to help create camaraderie, build relationships, and improve employee morale in Poughkeepsie from as far away as Beijing?

Globalization doesn't mean that one-on-one personal attention and caring will be less important. It's just the opposite. High-tech management will require high-touch human compassion and guidance more than ever before.

What Teams of the Future Will Need to Succeed 🔧TOOLS

In order to manage people globally and maintain their high morale, you and other leaders must be able to get together with your people online and review their work. Technology continually takes giant leaps forward, with software tools that let employees swap messages, trade documents, edit handouts, and even see and hear one another. Managers must stay abreast of technologies if they are to hash out ideas with workers in the UK, interview a new team member in Bangkok, review and edit some documents with a supervisor in Prague, get the latest update on a project from a team leader in San Diego, and kibitz a while with a new hire in Sydney.

The Glue That Bonds—Human Contact

No matter how hard you work to manage people globally, you'll find that keeping your people connected and working together across international and national boundaries is one tall order. And despite managers' increased reliance on warp-speed technology, there's nothing like old-fashioned one-on-one contact with people—shaking hands, smiling, chatting over coffee or tea, having lunch, and socializing in general.

So whenever possible—whether that's once a year, twice a year, or four times a year—plan to bring as many people together as you can. Pick a convenient location and have everyone meet there, in person. Maybe it's in Europe one year and in the U.S. the next. Even if you spend a few days wrestling with mediocre issues you've wrestled with over

Beware of Online Ping-Pong ⚠CAUTION! ⋀⋀

When workers are spread across the globe, setting a meeting time can be tricky at best, resulting in what's sometimes called "online ping-pong" and, therefore, massive confusion. To avoid the dreaded ping-pong match, start by selecting the people who should attend the online meeting, then pick a meeting time (taking time zones into consideration), and then send out a standard e-mail meeting invitation with as much notice as possible, making it easy for recipients to quickly accept or decline.

the Internet, the real value lies in the interaction among people who rarely see each other. Get-togethers like this become the social glue of global organizations. And managers worldwide attest to the power of the human connection.

What Managers Have to Say

One manager from Geneva says,

> We've been holding such events for our employees once a year for the past three years now. And over time we've seen the benefits mount. At some point during the get-together, a critical mass of connection takes place between everyone and you can just see it creating high employee morale and better, stronger networking with one another. That's something you just can't get in cyber-space alone.

If bringing people together from all parts of the world isn't feasible, then make your human connection felt via the Internet, as one woman from New York describes:

> Because I have a strong need to be connected to the organization and my people, I always let people know what's on my mind. I write a detailed e-mail to all of my employees twice a month. I let them know how I'm feeling about how the company is doing, or I'll discuss a particu-lar subject that's on everyone's minds. I may offer my perspective on a new business strategy we're considering implementing, or a new business model for our Southeast Asia office. My twice-monthly e-mail correspondence has become the glue that binds me closely to my people and a great way for me to help charge people up when I can't be right there with them.

The Americanization of Globalization

While you're still grappling with the promise and perils of glob-alization and what it requires of you as a leader of high morale and future thinking, I'll throw in another curve ball—the Americanization of globalization.

Here's the mind flip: 15 years ago business leaders assumed that in the 21st century Japan would be running the show. After all, the Japanese had perfected a business model that American companies were trying to emulate right and left. Now, fast-forward 15 years and—my, oh my, what a difference a few years can make! Today Japanese companies are trying to imitate their American rivals instead!

So what's going on? It's called the Americanization of the world and there are lots of examples to point to. Just take a look at all of the worldwide professional consultancy firms, like accounting and investment banking. The strongest global franchises belong to companies that have strong franchises in the U.S., like Ernst & Young and Deloitte & Touche. And it's no secret that American companies like Morgan Stanley and Goldman Sachs control the majority of the world's transactions when it comes to mergers and acquisitions. The message is this: if you're not strong in the U.S., it's tough to be strong anywhere else.

In short, to obtain a strong presence in the global marketplace, you simply must be a strong player in America. It's almost impossible to have a strong presence in other parts of the world if your company isn't strong economically in the U.S.

This isn't to say that managers should worry only about strengthening business in the U.S. It just points to the fact that what we're partially experiencing during this globalization process is the Americanization of the world economy. And that's something managers of companies large and small should be cognizant of.

Morale at the Speed of Change

A powerful global transformation has begun. Primarily due to the Internet, managers are discovering and inventing new ways to share their knowledge, hope, and enthusiasm with their employees at incredible speed. As a result, managers are getting smarter faster.

Our global society is requiring all managers to rise to a new level and start leading in brave new ways like never before. The emerging e-model of doing business is increasingly the norm. It's about being in sync with your people and with the overall goals of the organization second by second, rather than day by day. It's time to stop, breathe, and evaluate.

I Brake for Global Change

Maybe you remember a few years back when lots of people had bumper stickers on their cars that read, "I brake for children" or "I brake for bicycles" or even "I brake for whales." The original point of the popular campaign was that it's good to stop and consider what you're doing before you do something you may regret. The same principle applies here to the changes we as managers are encountering daily. Maybe it's time for all managers to wear bumper stickers that read, "I brake for change," so that they can stop and alert employees to what they may be anticipating on the horizon.

In Fast Times, Employees Don't Need to Be Managed

We're living in exciting times and globalization signifies yet more change coming our way. We're continually witnessing exploding technologies and new and improved knowledge on every level. And these changes are driving the fundamental ways we do business and, more important, the ways we manage our people.

And perhaps herein lies the real lesson for all managers—that we *can't* manage people. As managers and supervisors, all we can really do for people is to facilitate their success and hopefully influence their behaviors. We can even help co-create positive, healthy, and high-performing work environments, yes. But when it comes down to the nitty-gritty, people must manage themselves, their ideas, and, yes, even their morale, and then they must be held responsible and accountable for doing so.

Maybe it's time for all of us to stop for a moment in this high-speed world and brace ourselves for—you guessed it—

more change. And remember that in the midst of all that is going on around us, it's important for managers to maintain the human side of leadership, which includes compassion, love, and understanding for all people.

It's a Time for Managers to Act Swift and Be Brave

Globalization means more e-competition, crazy, new, and disruptive technologies, and rapidly changing business models—all of which are bound to impact your employees' morale. Therefore, it's time for managers to act swift and be brave. Anything less will surely result in being shoved aside by swifter, braver competitors.

Manager's Checklist for Chapter 2

❏ Globalization has become ingrained in our assumptions about how we do business, how we behave as managers, and how we treat our employees, both near and far.

❏ If your business can function using a computer and telephone line, then you're globally capable.

❏ Managers must learn to think globally and act locally.

❏ High morale is high morale anywhere you go in the world.

❏ Virtual teams are on the rise, as technology brings us more possibilities. The challenge is to manage them effectively.

❏ If you treat people like they are 10,000 miles away, they will feel 10,000 miles away.

❏ Even virtuality cannot replace the glue that bonds better than anything else—human contact.

❏ Managers are experiencing the Americanization of the world economy.

Keeping the People Who Keep Your Business in Business

There are two important management issues that are closely interconnected: employee retention and employee morale. If people are bailing out of the organization right and left, you can bet that employee morale is suffering. And if employee morale is pitifully low, it's a sure thing that people are looking for jobs elsewhere.

As a manager, you've probably experienced something similar to this scenario. After months of searching, you find someone who you think is going to be the perfect team leader for your marketing group, who will fire up the others and lead the way for the team to achieve all the goals in the marketing plan. So you schmooze this candidate, hire her, train her, and give the ultimate pep talk to your marketers about the great new person coming on board. When she does, she's in the position only three months before discovering what she believes to be greener pastures at Bigger Carrot, Inc. And poof! Say goodbye to Ms. Perfect-for-the-Marketing-Job and say hello to a team morale problem.

Free-agent worker Typically someone in their 20s or 30s, a free spirit in the workforce who won't hesitate to move from one job to another or even jump from one career to another when the urge strikes. This person might be VP of Talent at a *Fortune* 500 company one year and backpacking in the Himalayas the next. The mentality of the free-agent worker is that life is too short to spend it all in one spot and that security is just a superstition. Free-agent workers won't commit their loyalty to one company easily, but only if their values and personal needs are being respected and met.

When Poor Retention Bruises Morale

Employee retention is a significant factor that you can easily over-look when struggling to maintain morale, especially if you're managing young employees moving up the ranks. Employees in their 20s and 30s aren't buying into the I'll-work-here-until-I-retire myth. On top of that, job security is just a superstition to that generation of employees, who've witnessed firsthand the overnight death of dot-coms worldwide. These employees consider themselves to be "free-agent workers," not company "lifers" like their parents and their grandparents.

Expect Two to Three Years Max—or Offer Something Better

Most 20-somethings and 30-somethings are looking to make their mark fast and furious and then move on to something different and more challenging, which may or may not fall into the realm of the traditional workplace. These free-spirited workers often pull up stakes and do things like join the Peace Corps, start a business from home, or just freelance in the virtual work-place. Tom Peters warns that no employer should expect more than two good years out of any employee; to keep them longer than that, you'd better come up with something pretty damn extraordinary. It's that simple ... and it's that hard.

Make the Most of Their Time

John Patterson, Priceline.com's former vice president of talent (see, even the big shots don't always stick around forever!), shares the Tom Peters philosophy on what managers can realistically expect from today's employees. "Everyone is a temporary employee in this talent war," he points out. "It's your job to make sure each employee's two or three years on the job is as productive and as rewarding as possible." Maybe if more managers would adopt this attitude up front, they wouldn't be setting themselves up for the inevitable employee morale roller coaster ride.

Tough Managers Fight Back

Is there a way for a manager to fight back? Yes, just do your best. Hold on to your stars as long as you can. That's it. That's all you can do. If an employee gives you two great years, then fine, you got two productive years and so did the employee. If an employee gives you 20 years, then count your blessings, but just don't expect that to be the norm.

Employee retention experts agree that holding on to star performers as long as possible keeps workplace morale healthy and in balance. Experts also say that in order to keep the best-of-the-best, managers have to provide intangibles such as autonomy, purpose, and challenge—the preferred diet of the free-agent worker. It's the human side of doing business that keeps us all in business. It can be harder than it looks, but don't get discouraged. Learn from veteran managers who have developed a special knack for recruiting and retaining top talent.

Taking Care of Talent

Thomas Kasten worked for Levi Strauss & Co. for 33 years. In that time he learned a few things about getting, keeping, and growing employees. Kasten refers to this as "the care and feeding of talent." Like so many other managers who have been around for a while, Kasten knows that employees aren't attracted and retained by tangibles alone: "Compensation and benefits no longer dictate why and when a talented person joins or leaves a company," he asserts. Oh, sure, there are people who are strictly motivated by the almighty dollar, but those people are not the rule. The two most important factors, according to Kasten, are the quality of management and employees' ability to work on way-cool things.

Dignity and Respect ... and "Way-Cool Things"

Through the preshrunk peace-symbol jeans of the '60s, the corduroy and polyester bell bottoms of the '70s, the acid-washed look of the '80s, the Dockers™ of the '90s, or Levi's newest jeans for the 21st century, the designated Engineered Jeans™, one thing remains constant at Levi Strauss—workers at this multinational company love their jobs and have been assured by its leaders that every employee worldwide will receive dignity and respect based on the Levi Strauss code of conduct.

Ethical conduct and the responsibility to treat people fairly have characterized the way this authentic American icon has always done business. In 1994, Levi Strauss was named *Fortune* magazine's most admired apparel company and in 2000 it ranked second on the list of *Fortune*'s "America's Best Companies for Minorities." So updating the organization's recruiting and retention programs at the turn of the century was critical.

Kasten played a pivotal role in the process, so it's with good authority that he cites two factors as most important factors when it comes to keeping people:

- quality of management (that's you!)
- making it possible for employees to work on "way-cool things"

In other words, it's important for managers to match their employees' specific talents and interests to exciting or challenging new projects that ignite passion for the job.

Techniques for Keeping Employees

During his years of managing employees, Kasten came up with some powerful techniques for getting and keeping the best talent possible, even in the worst economic times. Here are a few morale-boosting suggestions you may want to adopt.

Chefs Light Their Fire

The regional VP for a chain of upscale Southwestern eateries directed all of his restaurant managers to rev up the morale of their executive chefs by transforming their kitchen duties and stimulating their creative juices. Each chef was challenged to come up with one new and exciting menu item that guaranteed to excite the taste buds of patrons and restaurant reviewers from Houston to Albuquerque. By combining their innate creativity with their experiences and cooking skills, all of the chefs reported a sense of renewal and excitement about their work. The idea worked so well that restaurant management made Cuisine Creations a monthly showcase of each house chef's specialty item on every menu. And when restaurant reviewers got wind of the inventive approach, they wrote newspaper and magazine articles touting the trendy restaurant chain and its creative chefs—which further boosted employee pride and morale.

Explain to employees how the business is run. In other words, teach them the biz. Show them the balance sheet and explain how to read it. Educate and engage your employees. Morale bumps up a notch when employees know how they're involved in the overall process and feel part of a bigger, more important picture. They're also less likely to leave.

Help employees find new jobs internally. Companies need to adjust jobs and to invite and encourage career changes internally. Today's free-agent workers want to feel free to move frequently between jobs, so why not just create those jobs internally for them and keep the best people from leaving the organization? (Read more about this in Chapter 4 on redesigning jobs.)

Treat people the way "they" want to be treated. Managers should send the message that says, "It's all about you, you, you." Not me, me, me. So don't treat employees the way you would want to be treated or even the way this book says to treat them. Treat them the way they want to be treated and watch people respond with commitment and loyalty to the company.

Have pizza and beer with your employees. Whether it's that fare or it's hamburgers and milkshakes or it's sushi and sake, the point

> ### Create New Jobs
> **TRICKS OF THE TRADE**
>
> Levi Strauss veteran Thomas Kasten helped create a "Talent Inventory" for the company that contained the name of every employee and his or her skills and interests. The database was then used, when the time was right, to help managers create new jobs for their employees based on those skills and interests. The advantages of keeping the most valuable people outweighed the inconvenience and cost of changing the organizational chart.

is to organize lots of after-work get-togethers and celebrations. By getting to know your employees, you'll be creating a climate of trust and gaining insights into your people—and that can be very valuable for any manager.

Mentor everyone. Forget the org charts. Let employees see how things really work firsthand. New employees want to see people in action, socializing, and interacting with each other in meetings or during lunch. Establish a buddy system and give new hires a sense of community and belonging as soon as they enter the new environment.

Buddy systems can also work well when helping someone get quickly acclimated to a new task. The buddy can demonstrate how the job is done, answer questions, coach, and help the person to become more confident.

> ### Don't Expect Every Player to Be a Cheerleader
> **CAUTION!**
>
> Managers must be sensitive to the diverse personalities of their employees. Take time to get to know your people. Ask them how they'd like to be treated and then respect their wishes. Remember: not all your employees are cheerleaders, nor do they want to be. That doesn't mean those people don't have high morale and feel enthusiastic about their work. It just means that they express their happiness and motivation differently.

Don't just *have* fun—*be* fun! All work and no play…. Well, you get the picture. At Levi Strauss, managers are encouraged to orchestrate employee outings, like attending San Francisco Giants baseball games or taking tours of Napa wine country. Fun in the workplace creates a culture of spontaneity

Everyone Needs a Buddy

Buddy systems (a.k.a. shadow programs, employee coaching, and mentoring) can be very beneficial for orientation and great for morale. It's easy to implement a buddy system. Simply assign a new employee to someone who's been around the company a while, to serve as the buddy. Like a big brother or big sister, the buddy helps make the new person's transition into the workplace easier by taking the rookie to meetings, introducing him or her to other employees, eating lunch together, and sharing experiences about the company and the job.

and creativity. When workers are having fun, they're energized and morale runs high. And then, when their managers join in with them, everything cranks up a notch—employees are motivated to do their best work.

Know the names of everyone who works for you. It doesn't matter if the work group consists of a few employees or a few hundred, managers should know them all.

From day one, be clear on your expectations. This is a key retention tactic that managers need to hone. From the start, new employees must understand what is expected of them and how

Smart Managers Know These Fun Facts

Companies who use fun to build morale and increase retention are aware of these fun facts:

- **Fact #1.** When people have fun on the job, there's often a reduction in overall stress, which means lower health care costs, less absenteeism, greater productivity, and improved morale.
- **Fact #2.** When an organization encourages workers to enjoy a sense of humor, they often respond with a more flexible approach to their work, which inspires more innovative and creative thinking.
- **Fact #3.** Humor helps lighten the load and unites people.
- **Fact #4.** Being silly can help employees put things into perspective. When people enjoy a healthy sense of humor about their work, it forces them to step back and see the big picture, usually more clearly. In the words of Austrian philosopher Ludwig Wittgenstein, "If people did not sometimes do silly things, nothing intelligent would ever get done."

Some Serious Advice About Fun

Keep in mind that what's fun for one person may not be
fun for another and what works for one organization's
culture may not be appropriate for another.

Look at the contrast between two highly successful airlines: Virgin
Atlantic and British Airways. Virgin is known for its zany, thrill-seeking
CEO (and hot-air balloonist) Richard Branson, who inspires lots of
fun, out-of-the-box, in-flight perks, such as magicians who entertain
passengers and masseuses for the travel weary—and not just in first
class. According to Branson, founder of Virgin's mega music stores,
"We're still in the entertainment industry at 25,000 feet." British
Airways, on the other hand, is far more traditional in how its people
celebrate their successes and conduct in-flight business—and they
don't care to be in the entertainment industry at all. That doesn't
mean that British Airways employees don't work in an enjoyable
atmosphere or have fun on the job.

To keep employees happy, you don't have to create a big-top circus
environment. What matters is that your employees enjoy what they're
doing.

their performance will be measured. Managers need to communicate those expectations right up front, succinctly and clearly if
they want new hires to become long-time, motivated employees.

**Make every resignation an opportunity for retention and
improved morale.** If you're not conducting employee exit interviews, then you may be missing out on the biggest opportunity

Master of Employee Relationships

Herb Kelleher, chairman of the board and former president
of Southwest Airlines, never ceases to amaze both internal
and external customers with his uncanny ability to remember the
names of everyone he's ever met. It wouldn't matter if Kelleher met
you in San Antonio or Seattle among throngs of people in a crowded
airport; if he met you once, he'd remember you when you ran into
him a year later at Love Field in Dallas. His extraordinary way with
people and his attention to what they care about continues to set him
apart from the pack. Note: his company is not small, with more than
33,000 employees.

10 Recommendations for Retention

Smart Managing
- Treat employees like partners.
- Communicate objectives and expectations clearly.
- Focus on managing performance, not controlling people.
- Empower your employees—trust their judgment and common sense.
- Take time to recognize the human needs of your people.
- Invest in your employees and encourage their personal and professional development.
- Place a premium on employee involvement, new ideas, and innovative techniques.
- Celebrate mistakes by tolerating intelligent errors and experimentation.
- Keep it fun.
- Have a reward system in place.

to retain top talent and boost workplace morale. The chances are good that departing employees will be forthcoming and honest about their reasons for leaving, since they're no longer depending on you for a paycheck. You can use any information gained through exit interviews to fight employee turnover, keep top talent in place, and bump up workplace morale.

Talent Crashes and Burnout

Let's face it: not every company or manager is up on what it takes to keep employees enthusiastically performing at their peak. Unfortunately, there are still plenty of employers out there who are still having a hard time understanding that some of the so-called "soft issues" really are important when it comes to promoting high morale and developing employees to perform to their full potential.

Even with all that we know about what employees need to thrive, be more productive, and work better, there are thousands of organizations that have not yet adapted to this reality. Their managers continue to look at people as parts of a machine. They can only associate their employees with costs, like overhead, compensation, benefits, etc. And to make matters worse, those managers have come to accept the high cost of turnover and low morale as the price they must pay for doing business. If these managers would just concentrate on hiring the best people, valuing them, and meeting their needs, they'd be saving millions of dollars over time. When talent crashes, costs soar.

> **Costs of Employee Turnover**
>
> Here's a formula for calculating the costs of employee turnover: Recruiting Expenses + Travel and Relocation Costs + Training and Administrative Costs + Loss of Productivity = $$$High Cost of Employee Turnover$$$

You are obviously not one of these managers—or you wouldn't be reading this book. Keep telling yourself that social change takes time. Heck, it takes centuries. But we're closer in the 21st century than we've ever been before to understanding the human condition at work and appreciating and valuing human capital. It's the holistic antidote for employee burnout and talent crashes.

Companies That Lead the Way

There are thousands of managers, just like you, in companies in every community on the globe, that have spent time building reputations for their companies as employers of choice. This chapter was written for managers like you who believe that it's worth building a reputation that says, "Everyone wants to work here."

One such company is SAS Institute of Cary,

> **Walk the Talk or Sacrifice Your Credibility**
>
> The results of one survey of executives suggest that claims that "our people are our greatest asset" may be just words. In the survey, nine out of 10 executives told researchers that their employees were their company's most important asset. However, when asked to rank seven key issues that determine an organization's success, the leaders ranked "people performance" sixth!
>
> Leaders must walk the talk. If you're going to claim that people are important, then back it up with action—or you risk losing credibility and respect.

How Do Employees Feel?

In a study of 3,000 employees, 56% said their companies failed to show concern for them, 45% said their companies failed to treat them fairly, and 41% said their employers failed to trust them. Only 24% of employees said they were "truly loyal" to their employers and planned to stay at least two years. How would *your* employees have responded to this survey?

North Carolina. SAS is a world leader in business intelligence software and service, serving more than 37,000 business, government, and university sites in 111 countries. SAS prides itself on treating its employees with respect. Every employee is nurtured like family and is treated with respect and care. SAS goes so far as to credit its success in direct proportion to the time and money invested in its people.

The Men's Wearhouse also believes that employees are worth the investment. The company provides training—lots of it. Each year hundreds of Men's Wearhouse employees, known as clothing consultants, attend its Suits High, Suits University, and Selling Accessories University training sessions, programs, and seminars in Fremont, California. New hires spend about four days in one of the 30 sessions held yearly at the corporate university. The cost to the company? A cool million. The return on investment? Super high employee morale (just go there and see for yourself) and lower turnover than its competitors. Training is worth the investment. In the words of the founder, George Zimmer, "I guarantee it!"

These are just two examples of companies that treat their employees well. Other leaders in this respect include USAA, Starbucks, Chick-fil-A, Nordstrom, and MBNA.

Hire the Right People

This isn't a book about how to interview or hire employees, but it's important to devote a few pages to interviewing and hiring the right people, because if managers hired the right people, morale and retention would be far less a problem.

> ### Hire with Chutzpah!
> A manager's hiring mistakes are tomorrow's turnovers. More than 20% of employees are poor or lower than aver-age performers; bad hiring decisions are the reason. Bad hiring deci-sions are also the reason that only 50% of new employees last six months on the job. Too many managers are not taking enough respon-sibility for hiring. Too many managers are hiring the "best of the worst" just because they think good people are in short supply. It's time for managers to put some chutzpah back into hiring.

If the right people aren't hired, you as the manager are responsible for dealing with the headaches. That means that right here, right now, you have to claim pri-mary responsibility for the hiring decisions—not the team and not HR.

> **Chutzpah** The Yiddish word for supreme self-con-fidence, nerve, audacity, guts. Chutzpah is the perfect term and atti-tude for managers to adopt when it comes to taking back the interviewing and hiring process.

Attitude—What You See Is What You'll Get

So what can managers do to control today's hiring mistakes that quickly become tomorrow's turnover casualties? Well, for starters you can read *Hiring Great People* by Kevin C. Klinvex, Matthew S. O'Connell, and Christopher P. Klinvex (McGraw-Hill, 1999). But there's a rule of thumb that you can put into prac-tice immediately. It's a standard by which the best-of-the-best organizations hire their people, organizations that report the lowest turnovers rate in their respective industries. The rule: hire for attitude and train for skill. The reason: what people know is often far less important than what they are.

So which organizations are hiring for attitude? Nordstrom, Whole Foods Market, Nucor Corporation, Rosenbluth International, and Southwest Airlines, to name a few. All of these organizations subscribe to the belief that people with the right attitude can always be trained in matters they need to learn. However, a bad attitude is something you cannot easily untrain. This is why some organizations begin to gauge a candidate's attitude from the moment he or she walks through the door. Receptionists are great at sizing up a person's attitude and demeanor before the interview and then reporting to managers. Do you ask your receptionist for input on candidates?

Four Steps to Smarter Hiring

Hire for attitude and train for skill. Attitude is the most important criterion for most jobs. Even in highly technical or scientific jobs, statistics prove over and over that having the right attitude is directly related to strong performance.

Practice the Popeye Principle. The cartoon character was probably right when he said, "I yam what I yam," and so most likely are your job candidates. Never hire someone on the belief that he or she can be changed. It's a fatal mistake.

Let behavior predict behavior. The best predictor of future behavior is past behavior. This is not to say that people do not grow or improve over time, but a manager can get a good feel for how someone will act in future situations by examining that person's actions in similar past situations.

Simulate the job. BMW built a simulated assembly line just for this purpose. If job candidates cannot perform several job-related tasks that meet the strict requirements of the job, they are not hired.

Audition for Attitude

Your organization will flourish, profit, perform beyond your greatest expectations, and exude

---

TRICKS OF THE TRADE

Interviewing Tip

Never ask theoretical questions in an interview. For example, a question like "What would you do if ...?" only invites a candidate to exaggerate or imagine his or her abilities. The rule here is to *stay out of the 'woulds.'* Instead, probe into the candidate's experience: "When have you worked under a lot of pressure to meet a deadline and then missed it? Tell me the circumstances and what you learned from the experience." Remember: you're looking for desirable behaviors and attitudes that identify star talent.

excitement, enthusiasm, and passion—provided you hire winners, promote winners, and keep those winners as long as possible.

According to consultant T. Scott Gross, author of *Outrageous! Unforgettable Service ...Guilt-Free Selling* (AMACOM, 1998), every interview should be an extraordinary audition. Why? Because auditions create competitive spirit and enthusiasm for the job and they give the potential employee a shot at demonstrating his or her employee morale in action. It's a performance, after all, and talent rules at an audition!

Set up auditions so that candidates exhibit behaviors required for the job. If the job requires selling, you might ask candidates to introduce themselves, the company, and some products or services. If the job requires handling customer questions and complaints, you might ask some employees to play the part of customers, to test the candidates under fire. If the job requires basic skills—math, computer, writing, or whatever—you can test those skills in a realistic setting.

Auditioning for High Morale

TRICKS OF THE TRADE

Suppose that you're hiring a marketer for Hoola Hoops R Us. During your usual interview process, you determine that a candidate's basic qualifications, competencies, and personality all look fine, but you really need someone in this position who's filled with high energy and bursting with gusto about marketing your hoops to Baby Boomers' babies. How do you know the candidate has what it takes to sustain his or her motivation and morale over the long haul?

Morale-boosting guru T. Scott Gross recommends asking candidates to audition. You can do this in various ways.

One way is to have the candidate deliver lines from a monologue you've prepared, either straight from your script or personalized to make them sing with enthusiasm and passion for the job. A monologue might start out like this: "Hi, my name is _____ and I can't wait to tell you all about my job here at Hoola Hoops R Us ...."

Then, watch candidates soar with the opportunity to really turn it on or buckle under the pressure. All of a sudden, enthusiasm for the job isn't so hard to measure, is it?

Gross cautions not to use the term "role play." He believes that for many people this term suggests that the situation is much less serious than if you phrase it as an opportunity for candidates to show their skills.

This chapter has provided you with some of the guiding principles of employee retention and some techniques and tools you can start using right away. Remember: the sooner you focus on keeping the people who keep your business in business, the sooner you'll be revving up employee morale.

Manager's Checklist for Chapter 3

❑ Free-agent workers won't easily commit their lives to one company. If they do, it's because their values and personal needs are being respected and met.

❑ Employee retention experts agree that holding onto star performers for as long as possible keeps workplace morale healthy and in balance.

❑ Match employees' talents and interests with challenging new projects that excite and ignite passion for the job.

❑ Help employees find new jobs—internally.

❑ Treat people the way *they* want to be treated, not the way *you* would want to be treated.

❑ Don't expect every employee to be a cheerleader.

❑ Make an employee's resignation your company's greatest opportunity for retention and improved morale.

❑ If you're going to claim that people are your most important asset, then back it up with action or face losing credibility.

❑ Audition job candidates for their enthusiasm and positive morale.

❑ Hire the right people by hiring for attitude and training for skill.

To Boost Morale, Alter the Environment

As a manager or supervisor, you are capable of having an enormous effect on your company's work environment. According to the basic principles of environmental psychology, the actual setting or work environment can have a dramatic impact on overall employee morale, enthusiasm for the job, and productivity. Managers and supervisors need to be aware of this and do what they can to enhance the work environment whenever and in whatever way possible.

Love Your People and They'll Love Where They Work

Managers must be willing to make time to alter the environment if and when necessary. And it's easier to do than you may think.

Contrary to popular belief, altering the work environment to encourage and support more positive and high-performing employees isn't about spending a lot of money or having fancy digs. That's not what makes people love where they work. So it doesn't matter if your company is located on the penthouse floor

Environmental psychology A course of academic study, encompassing a range of disciplines that relate to employee behaviors, stresses, anxieties, likes and dislikes, and physiological changes on the job, such as heart rate and blood pressure.

of the most upscale skyscraper in town, if your building was designed by an award-winning architect and built from the finest steel, chrome, and glass, or if your offices have the loveliest landscaping and the most extraordinary fountains and marble floors in the entry way. That's not the kind of environment I'm talking about. Why? Because none of that matters if the managers and supervisors who reside there do not genuinely care for and love their people.

When I talk about altering the environment, I mean altering workplace behaviors and improving the way that leaders communicate with and treat their people. Sure, it's nice to work in fine surroundings, but creating high employee morale is not

⚠ CAUTION!

Beware of Posh Surroundings

A former manager for a communications company in Mountain View, California, warns of posh surroundings where there is no substance:

When I went to work for this firm, I've got to admit, I was pretty taken in by the looks of everything. The building was new and the offices we had on the two top floors were quite the showplace. The artwork on the walls was commissioned by well-known artists and the marble entry way was actually flown in from Italy. I went home and told my wife, "You can't believe the beautiful office I work in!" But it wasn't long before I got the real picture. By all appearances we were a hotshot communications firm, but within those walls we were a company of people who were morally, emotionally, and synergistically bankrupt.

Now I'm working for a company with a far more humble office setting, but internally we are a synergistic, highly motivated, morale-driven, high-energy work group. You can feel the energy in the air around here and management makes everyone feel important and valued. I never thought I'd say this about my work environment, but I really do love working here.

about art deco furniture and pretty wallpaper. The message is this: love your people and they'll love where they work.

Managers caring about people at every level in the organization, treating them with respect and dignity, and caring about their families is often enough to create an atmosphere that nurtures joy, employee satisfaction, and higher employee morale.

Spruce It Up and Shine It Up

Making people feel as comfortable as possible at work is a good thing. So invite employees to polish up their work areas. If you don't have the budget to hire someone to make that happen, ask your employees if they'd like to pitch in and help make their workspaces more enjoyable, livable, inspirational, uplifting, and brighter. Most managers quickly discover that employees will jump at the chance to make their environment more attrac-

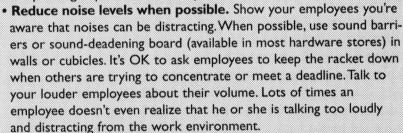

Pointers on Altering the Environment

Here are some tips for altering the work environment for a more pleasing experience for everyone.

- **Reduce noise levels when possible.** Show your employees you're aware that noises can be distracting. When possible, use sound barriers or sound-deadening board (available in most hardware stores) in walls or cubicles. It's OK to ask employees to keep the racket down when others are trying to concentrate or meet a deadline. Talk to your louder employees about their volume. Lots of times an employee doesn't even realize that he or she is talking too loudly and distracting from the work environment.
- **Give 'em their space.** If you can't alter or enlarge the spatial area around each employee, then at least try to maintain some areas of large, uncluttered, open space, where employees can go to take a breather. A larger, less cluttered space gives people a feeling of relaxation and counteracts any feelings of claustrophobia.
- **Cheer things up.** If the workspace is getting a little old and looking run down, ask employees if they'd like to have a work party to brighten things up. You'd be surprised what a fresh coat of paint, some cool picture frames, and a simple window treatment or two can do to calm nerves, reduce stress, and create a generally more pleasing environment—and all for a reasonable amount of money.

tive and be involved with the décor and overall improved appearance of their workspaces—even if they're the ones doing the sprucing.

Keep It Interesting—Redesign Jobs

What do employees want? They want good jobs that keep their interests high and maximize their talents and abilities. They want jobs that will help them to develop and fulfill their greatest potential. And when they find themselves in undesirable, dead-end jobs, they will most likely disconnect or leave.

Like anything else, jobs can get stagnant, so managers need to come up with inventive new ways to redesign jobs if they are to keep their stars and motivate them to perform at their personal best.

One manager who's mastered the technique of job redesign is Jeff Jobe, General Manager of Portland's trendy, upscale Heathman Hotel. In an effort to keep things creative, interesting, and more efficient for guests, Jobe says, "We literally blew up our front desk consoles and then eliminated three key positions all at once." The key positions are bellman, concierge, and front-desk person. According to Jobe, the dramatic workplace changes created an even more desirable opportunity for those whose positions were slashed.

"From the three positions we eliminated, we created one really great position called 'Personal Concierge,'" says Jobe. "You can say we allowed our employees to automatically upgrade themselves and their previous jobs by taking on a more specialized job with greater combined responsibility." It takes just one person, in the newly designed position, to encompass all of the following responsibilities: checking guests in faster and with greater ease, escorting them with their baggage to their rooms, and then providing each guest with a business card and letting him or her know that the staff member will be that guest's personal concierge for the entire stay.

Jobe says the success of redesigning his employees' jobs, as well as the Heathman's traditional work environment, rests in

---

Building an Upgradeable Staff

Jeff Jobe offers some advice for redesigning people's jobs, while helping everyone become upgradeable in their positions.

- Practice the 3 C's: creative commitment to customer service.
- Communicate with everyone directly.
- Provide extensive employee training and development.
- Set up discussion groups where employees can ask questions and make recommendations to management.
- Ask "What if?" questions.
- Ask, "In order to do this, we must (have employees fill in the blank) do what?"
- Create ongoing opportunities for people to improve themselves.

---

three main areas—69 hours of "Personal Concierge" training, keeping employees well-informed of all changes that are about to take place, and inviting each employee to be a part of designing the way new roles will play out at the hotel in real situations. Employees at the Heathman have a significant say in hotel operations, ranging from compensation matters to building better internal customer service relationships.

Tips and Techniques for Redesigning Jobs

Variety Is the spice of life—mix it up. Whenever possible, keep jobs multi-task and multi-talent driven. Workers want to do an assortment of things when they're at work. Typically, the more skills required to do a job, the more satisfied the worker, hence higher employee morale and motivation.

The kicker is finding the right combination of talents that an employee enjoys doing and then matching those talents to the needs of the job. This can sometimes be tougher for people who are performing specialized kinds of jobs. That's when you'll have to put on your thinking cap and come up with new ways to make those jobs more varied as well. Better yet, why don't you ask your employees to suggest a desired mix of skills and activities that may make doing a very specialized job more interesting? For example: A health care worker may start providing more aspects of patient care and as a result have fewer patients but a wider variety of tasks that keep the job more interesting. This beats having several health-care workers all performing just one or two tasks for a multiple of people over and over again, which could quickly become repetitive and mundane.

Detail the purpose and pride associated with the job. As the manager, it's important that you convey to your work group the larger purpose of their efforts. If that's not evident upfront, employees may never see the greater purpose of their work. One way to do this is to stress the true significance of a job and its specific impact on the lives of others, whether those are people within or outside the organization. Of course this can be easier to accomplish if your workers are assembling wheelchairs or are on the assembly line filling vials for an asthma medication. It's clear in these circumstances just how much the recipients of these efforts will greatly benefit and, as a result, be able to live more productive lives.

However, if your workers are doing something that isn't as easy to assign social and life-saving significance to, then you or someone else will have to explain it to them. Perhaps the greatest significance is in producing a higher quality product, meeting stakeholders' needs, or maintaining greater profits for the company so that workers can continue to receive better benefits or donate time and money to the company cause. Whatever the reason, look for and explain the purpose and pride behind the work to all of your employees. People want to know that their contributions, no matter how large or small, mean something.

Give people more responsibility, not just more work. Let employees take more responsibility for setting their own work schedules, coming up with their own work methods, deciding on standards of excellence, and then determining when they've achieved them. Give them the right to decide when to take breaks and even when to start and stop work. The objective here is to enrich their work with empowerment and authority. It's not about handing off more tasks. Responsibility enriches jobs and builds employee morale.

Ben & Jerry's Puts Global Purpose into Making Ice Cream

Ben & Jerry's Statement of Mission consists of three inter-related parts—product, economic, and social. Everyone in the organization is committed to the social statement and derives from it a sense of global purpose and pride.

Here's how it's done: 7.5% of pretax profits are committed to philanthropy and hundreds of grassroots organizations that specifically work toward progressive, worldwide social changes. Each employee in the socially conscious and politically active organization knows that his or her contribution goes toward helping a wide number of environmentally and socially responsible organizations. It's from this commitment that every employee feels a sense of meaning and purpose because they know their work at Ben & Jerry's contributes directly to making the world a healthier, more humane place to live and work.

Here is a list of just some of the social causes that the Ben & Jerry's organization has supported over the years with its generous grants:
- Dave Matthews Band and SaveOurEnvironment.org
- Children's Defense Fund
- Coalition for Environmentally Responsible Economics
- Business for Social Responsibility
- Center for Young Women's Development
- Senior Action Network
- Black Workers for Justice
- Bay Area Nuclear Waste Coalition
- Post Graduate Center for Mental Health
- Environmental Research Foundation
- Support Committee for Maquiladora Workers
- Farmworker Institute for Education and Leadership Training
- Klamath Siskiyou Wildlands Center

It's important to note that Ben & Jerry's was acquired by Unilever in April 2000 and Unilever has continued to honor Ben & Jerry's social commitment to making the world a better place to live.

Encourage employees to get cozy with customers. Managers can't be effective if they're paranoid about workers getting too close to their customers. For employees who want to hone their interpersonal skills, increased customer contact will sharpen their ability to troubleshoot problems, solve customer com-

Smart Managing

Ben & Jerry's Social Mission

The following is the social part of the Ben & Jerry's Statement of Mission:

To operate the Company in a way that actively recognizes the central role that business plays in the structure of society by initiating innovative ways to improve the quality of life of a broad community—local, national, and international.

plaints, develop solutions, and manage customer relationships—all great ways to establish closer customer ties and get valuable feedback for the company, not to mention developing a more varied skill set.

Give them freedom to care and to grow. Liberate your employees from management's authority whenever possible. Redesign jobs to build in greater independence and autonomy. Let common sense and good judgment be the cornerstones of decision-making. When employees take on personal responsibility, they become more accountable and more interested in their jobs. But when they're stifled and micromanaged, their spirit for the job slowly dies.

Enrich the Environment with Creative Benefits

Another way to reshape or enrich the environment is to enhance the benefits of working there. The days when benefits packages included nothing more than a health plan and dental coverage are—yawn—over. Managers are getting more and more creative in providing their employees with perks uniquely their own that contribute to an ever-changing, exciting, and high morale work environment.

Perks That Reshape and Enrich World-Class Companies

Here are a few examples:

Goldman Sachs, New York—When employees work late into the night, the Wall Street firm sends them home in a limo at no cost.

Valassis Communications, Livonia, Michigan—The company gives employees "wheels on loan" if their car is in the shop, "you've got it maid" discounts on maid service, and infant car seats to new parents.

MBNA, Wilmington, Delaware—Employees who say, "I do" receive generous wedding gifts from the firm, including limo service on their wedding day, $500, and a week of vacation. Other employee perks that enhance the workplace include on-site dry cleaning, shoe repair, and salon services.

WRQ, Inc., Seattle, Washington—Quirky but true, this integration software provider offers employees a nap room with futons and dock space for their kayaking commuters—a useful benefit in the great Northwest.

Edward Jones, St. Louis, Missouri—New moms don't sacrifice money for maternity leave. For six weeks after delivery, the investment firm pays 75% of a broker's average commissions for the previous half year.

J.M. Smucker, Orrville, Ohio—The famous jam maker enriches the environment with ongoing job rotations to keep employees motivated and interested.

BMC Software, Houston, Texas—No dress codes, no titles on doors, no assigned parking spaces. The result? No uptight hierarchy or top-down management.

Qualcomm, San Diego, California—This tech company gives $250 of support for any employee's kid who plays on a sports team and it also allows employees to accumulate as much unused vacation time as they like.

REI, Kent, Washington—New dads get two-weeks paid leave to be with their babies.

American Cast Iron Pipe, Birmingham, Alabama—This company features convenience for workers by housing an on-site clinic with primary-care physicians and dentists, to provide free medical and dental services for company employees, retirees, and their family members.

Capital One, Falls Church, Virginia—Employees' first year on the job earns them three weeks' paid vacation.

Dell Computer, Round Rock, Texas—The company gives every employee a week off at Christmas and 10 paid days a year for personal use.

AFLAC, Columbus, Georgia—Employees can take 12 weeks at full pay to care for a sick child, spouse, or parent.

Scitor Corporation, Sunnyvale, California—The company lets its people choose their own titles, reshaping the way employees think about themselves and their work.

Rodale, Emmaus, Pennsylvania—The publisher of living healthy books and magazines practices what it preaches by giving employees their own gardening plots on Rodale land.

Janus, Denver, Colorado—A generous time-off policy, free Starbucks coffee, and an ultra comfortable dress code make life at Janus pretty cushy.

Life Balance Keeps Employee Morale High

What's really going on here is that employers are making diligent efforts to help their employees balance their personal and business lives by making their work environment more enriching and satisfying.

So, as a manager, what's in it for you? A lot. Research continues to show that when employers give to their employees, their employees reward them with higher performance and productivity. According to Jack Hawley, author of *Reawakening the Spirit in Work* (Berrett-Koehler, 1993), "Workers always give to the organization or firm in direct proportion to what they perceive themselves receiving from it."

Year after year, managers come up with new and creative ideas that help reshape and enrich the work environment for their employees. Ask your employees to help add to the list.

Get to the Bottom of What People Need—Ask!

To find out what your people really need to alter the environment in a more positive way or to uncover what's necessary to enrich their jobs, all you may have to do is simply ask. You may be surprised to find out that most requests you will get are very easy to honor.

For example, the manager of the kitchen staff at an upscale resort in Kauai, Hawaii, was relieved to know he could easily

Most Requested Perk—Flexibility.
Managers who expect to succeed in maintaining high
employee morale will have to be flexible. Here's the kind of
flexibility employees ask for the most. Top picks include...
* Telecommuting
* Flexible schedules
* Job sharing
* Compressed workweek (10-hour days, four days a week)
* Reduction in summer work hours
* Time off for personal business when necessary

fulfill his employees' requests. According to the kitchen staff, all
they needed to make the environment easier to work in and
more enjoyable was a new set of kitchen knives and a larger,
more durable blender. That was it! Just two things and the manager was able to quickly and easily upgrade the kitchen's work
environment.

By trying to satisfy your employees' needs, you'll be
building higher employee
morale, which inevitably
contributes to lots of positive energy, which in turn
becomes synergy, meaning
that the members of the
team accomplish more
together than they would
divided. When this hap-
pens you'll be maximizing
and improving the environment for everyone.

Environmental synergy
The result of environmental
interactions that make the
whole greater than the sum of its
parts, allowing team members to
accomplish more together than they
could separately. Synergy helps develop a healthier work environment
where everyone feels more comfortable in times of both harmony and
conflict. With environmental synergy,
together everyone achieves more!

The Most Powerful Way to Improve the Environment—Train Everyone!

The Container Store in Dallas, Texas, gives its employees more
than 100 hours of training a year. Edward Jones initiates new
brokers with 17 weeks of classes and study sessions. And

Marriott thinks readiness is key, so it prepares workers at all levels for advancement with continuous cross-training programs.

Training isn't a frill to these companies or others like them—it's a necessity. And their high morale environments are a constant reminder of their commitment to people development as a worthwhile investment.

There are many good reasons to invest in training. Here are just a few of the most important reasons why managers should look to training in order to improve and crank up workplace morale.

- Training builds confidence and esteem. By training employees, managers are saying that their people are worth the investment.
- Training gives people the skills they need to succeed and develop.
- Training helps employees and companies keep pace with ongoing change.
- Training attracts talent and retains talent.
- Training contributes directly to customer satisfaction and ultimately company profits.

Training as a Holistic Concept

Employee learning and development is now being viewed in some organizations as a holistic concept, which means taking into consideration the whole person's mental, physical, emotional, and social well-being.

This approach also requires that training no longer be considered a one-time event that falls solely on the shoulders of management. A holistic or whole-person approach asks that employees focus on the value of *lifelong learning* rather than taking the myopic view of *lifetime employment.* Doing this requires that employees make a paradigm shift in their thinking, from "Train me" to "I'm responsible for my own lifelong learning and well-being, so I will take the initiative to become a continuous and intentional learner whenever possible."

A holistic approach to training honors and respects the

whole person and his or her responsibility to be accountable for seeking and taking advantage of continuous learning opportunities. It then becomes the manager's job to facilitate his or her workers' success and guide them toward those opportunities when possible.

Taking a Holistic and Whole-Person Approach

No longer can organizations and their leaders afford to compartmentalize their employees' lives. Drawing an invisible line that suggests a worker leave his or her personal and emotional life at the door when reporting for work ignores every aspect of humanness. That line from yesteryear's management rules is now outdated and blurred.

We know that it is impossible for an employee to close off parts of his or her personal life when coming to work. Why? Because that kind of behavior goes against human nature. The holistic approach to managing inspires positive employee morale by recognizing that one dimension of a person's life is affected by all the other dimensions and that the professional and personal lives of employees are closely connected. That's what I mean by the term "whole person."

Managers who are willing to take a more holistic and whole-person approach to creating a high morale workplace are often better able to appreciate and utilize their worker's human qualities.

To be able to inspire and lead others to perform at higher levels, you will first have to plug into your employees' human side, affirm them, and help them to meet their desires and needs on all levels. This is what makes the whole-person approach to managing and training both holistic and soulful.

What's Good for the Soul Is Good for the Work Environment

In their book, *The Soul at Work* (New York: Simon & Schuster, 2000), Roger Lewin and Birute Regine write of the powerful ways that managers are learning to respect the soul of the

The Human Side of Management Recognizes the Whole Person

Managing and supervising is about embracing the humanness of people. It's vital that managers recognize the value of people as human beings first and foremost and not look upon their workers as simply revenue producers. In other words, managers must nurture their nature.

The whole-person approach to training and managing others consists of four human parts that represent the qualities, skills, knowledge, and feelings organizations and their managers must recognize:

- *Head:* A person's head represents knowledge, unique expertise, intellectual property (i.e., patents, trade secrets, etc.), empowerment, competencies, attitude, motivation, character, integrity, and values.
- *Hands:* A person's hands are representative of specific skill sets, the implementation of those skills, follow-through, hands-on coaching, customer service, production, and manufacturing of company products.
- *Heart:* An employee's heart signifies caring, emotional depth, the ability to love and be loved, feelings, intuition, servant leadership, emotional intelligence, pride, spirit, and hope for a better tomorrow.
- *Feet:* The feet represent the foundation upon which the organization and its leadership are built. They also represent the organization's one-of-a-kind culture, history, traditions, company founders, organizational stability, and readiness to move forward and embrace change.

These four parts of the whole person, all together, represent the soul of the organization.

organization, as well as the souls of their workers.

This somewhat new and powerful way of thinking is more human-oriented and breeds greater success and higher morale in the workplace by creating an atmosphere of honest relationships and mutual respect. The words of Peter Senge sum it up best: "As we enter the twenty-first century, it is timely, perhaps even critical, that we recall what humans have understood for a very long time,

Key Term

Soul of the organization A concept that speaks to the spirit felt within an organization, its deeper meaning and purpose, the passion within each person, and the synergy among managers and their staff.

that working together can indeed be a deep source of meaning in our lives. Anything less is just a job."

Perceptive managers know that there's a huge discrepancy between the levels of employee morale in an organization with soul and the levels of employee morale in one without it. The organization with soul respects and treats its employees as whole persons. The other, without soul, treats people as mechanical producers of tasks for which they are compensated. Managers must work to close the gap in workplace behaviors between these two distinctly different work environments, because the soul of the organization is directly affected by the environmental behaviors that go on around it and vice versa.

Manager's Checklist for Chapter 4

❑ According to the basic principles of environmental psychology, the work environment can have a dramatic impact on overall employee morale, enthusiasm for the job, and productivity.

❑ Love your people and they'll love where they work.

❑ Managers caring about employees and their families is often enough to create an atmosphere that nurtures joy, employee satisfaction, and higher employee morale.

❑ Typically, the more skills required to do the job, the more satisfied the worker.

❑ When jobs become stagnant, redesign them.

❑ Enrich the environment by getting creative with employee benefits.

❑ If you want to improve the environment—train everyone!

❑ Consider training as a holistic concept.

❑ Managers must relate to the whole person: head, hands, heart, and feet.

❑ The soul of an organization is directly affected by its environment and vice versa.

Putting the Kibosh on Negativity

There's only one surefire way to know if employee morale is really positive and strong throughout your company—ask the people who actually work there. If negativity is seeping in, then it's time to put an end to all de-motivators in a hurry!

It's amazing how many managers and supervisors don't believe that it's possible to measure morale. Companies spend millions measuring every other aspect of their businesses, from customer satisfaction to return on investment, from employee performance to employee retention, but when it comes to measuring employee morale—nothing! Managers probably think that morale is something intangible. Not true. It can be measured—and what gets measured is what gets done, just as in any other area of your business.

Dangers of Not Measuring Employee Morale

It's dangerous when managers don't take time to measure morale in their companies. For instance, managers may take high employee morale for granted, especially when it's up and things are going great. When things appear to be going smoothly, managers may stop focusing on the little things that keep the ball rolling. They may stop asking questions, too. Therefore, they can miss the most ideal opportunities to fix employee dissatisfaction and problems quickly and inexpensively. When a manager allows employee morale to go unaudited, the little problems just grow over time.

Let's face it: effective managers have lots to do, constantly having to be sure that good systems are in place and running smoothly. But when things are running without a hitch, you can forget to check the system. After a while, you just stop thinking about the things that appear to be going well—like employee morale. And so you don't think to make sure that certain procedures are still serving their original, designated purposes.

It's a common dilemma that all managers face at one time or another in their careers. So the only way to avoid the low-employee morale trap is to conduct morale audits periodically. This way you're taking the pulse and the temperature of the organization on an ongoing basis to find out just what your employees are feeling and thinking. In other words, how they're really doing.

Auditing Employee Morale

Every organization depends on high employee morale to drive its progress and sustain its long-term survival. To quickly and easily assess your organization's employee morale status, use this measurement tool to get some fast answers.

First, managers and supervisors should complete the morale audit, then employees. Compare responses and see where discrepancies might be happening between managers and staff and get a clear picture of where you need to close the gap.

Use the following morale audit to fit the specific needs of your organization or your work group. You may have to modify certain questions to eliminate ambiguities or address industry-specific areas. But this should give you a good prototype from which to begin a surveying process. The survey should be completed anonymously and taken on the job.

	All the Time	Usually	Occa-sionally	Are You Kidding?
1. Managers and supervisors consistently express enthusiasm and excitement about the organization and its people.				
2. At work, everyone's opinions count.				
3. High employee morale is present throughout the organization. It can be felt.				
4. Programs are in place that contribute to employees' personal and professional growth.				
5. About every six months, someone talks to you about your personal or professional development.				
6. Creativity and fun are welcome in the organization.				
7. Leaders walk the talk at every level of the organization.				
8. Employees are valued, respected, and treated with dignity.				
9. There is a can-do attitude among employees.				
10. Philosophies and core values of the organization are not only lauded but practiced.				
11. You have the opportunity at work, at some point every day, to do what you do best.				
12. You get a sense of purpose and enjoyment from your work most days.				
13. For those interested in becoming a leader in the company, you believe there is ample opportunity to become one.				

Figure 5-1. Morale audit

Morale Audit Reveals Low Employee Satisfaction

Robert Johnson, a manager in a Detroit manufacturing plant says,

> By all appearances, morale seemed great around here. Of course, I was going by my gut feelings until I was given a baseline of specific feedback to work from. That's what conducting a morale audit did for us and that's when the fog lifted. I had no idea that a large percentage of my workers felt that management was uninterested in their ongoing personal or professional development. When I saw this, I immediately put into action a career counseling program to help remedy those feelings. The result was improved employee morale, which was reflected in the follow-up audit we did six months later. I'm convinced that employee morale can and should be measured regularly.

Any check marks in the "Occasionally" category indicate gaps or discrepancies in the system that should be examined. Any check marks in the "Are you kidding?" category flag serious concerns about low-employee morale in a particular area that require immediate attention from a manager or supervisor.

What to Do When Employee Morale Starts Ailing

When an audit reveals that employee morale may be ailing, then it's time to call in the morale doctors.

An organization in Salt Lake City, Utah, did this when its morale audit indicated that more than 40% of the employees felt that their opinions didn't count and another 43% believed that they had little chance of being promoted into a leadership position within the organization. So managers in the organization decided to set up an Employee Satisfaction Committee, also known as "morale doctors," to help uncover employee morale problems before they got out of hand. Management was soon inundated with volunteers to take on the job. They selected 12 people, representing different departments, to serve on the popular committee. Their assignment? To ensure that employee morale improved, specifically in the areas where the audit

Stopping Bigger Problems

To keep small problems and concerns from growing, an employee satisfaction committee can be extremely effective in remedying low-morale on the job.

One committee member at a biotech firm in Palo Alto, California, said that it didn't take him long to get to the bottom of a problem that affected employee morale:

All I did was ask and promise an update on progress, not even a solution, just an update, and employees were happy to oblige. One of our engineers thought that his suggestions were deemed useless by management. When I got to the bottom of the problem I determined that his recent suggestions were indeed solid and could save us all time and money. Upper management just got too busy to handle it. I took it to the committee, the changes were implemented that week, and the employee's morale shot through the roof! I really think we were on the verge of losing this guy.

reflected problems. Improvement was significant when measured the next time the company conducted the survey.

Auditing employee morale is the obvious first step managers should take when it comes to heading off potential workplace morale problems and dealing with employee negativity.

Top Three Negativity Invaders

One chapter can't begin to cover all of the hundreds of things that can undermine workplace morale—poor attitudes, mistreatment of employees by management, lack of respect, cynical and negative people, events, announcements, management decisions, disappointments, lack of praise and rewards, and so forth. So let's focus on the three negativity invaders that are most common and somehow seem to make their way into the workplace again and again:

- Fear
- Dreaded performance reviews
- Cynical attitudes

By becoming more aware of these three, you'll be better equipped to deal with them head on.

> ### Warning Signs That Negativity Is Creeping In
> • The "I can'ts" become frequent and addictive.
> • Employees spend too much conversational time criticizing others or the organization.
> • Employees behave with animosity.
> • Enjoyment and enthusiasm are lacking.
> • Each new idea or program is greeted with a "This too shall pass" attitude.
> • People seem fearful.
> • No one's laughing. There are no signs of fun.

Fear

Fear is paralyzing. It feeds on everything that brings out the worst in people. When fear sets in, it's usually a sign that management hasn't done its part to build confidence or tell employees everything there is to know. It can also be a sign that management is actually using fear as a tool to manipulate employees to work harder or do things a certain way because they fear the consequences. In fact, some leaders use fear to motivate— "Get the job done on time or you're fired!" But it's only weak and ineffective leaders who use fear to get people to perform. Smart leaders know that employee incentives and a promise for personal growth and development are the best motivators.

Fear is a serious negativity invader. One way to keep it from creeping into your workplace is to understand what employees fear most and then address those fears upfront, open and honestly, with everyone.

What employees fear the most:

1. That they will be rejected or not belong.
2. That they will be seen as vulnerable or weak.
3. That they won't measure up and, therefore, will appear inferior.

By having this information up front, managers and supervisors can find ways to overcome the most common employee fears.

When Fear Is Used to Motivate

There's probably no better example of fear in the workplace than in the 1952 episode of the *I Love Lucy* show, called "Job Switching"—better known as "the Candy Factory." In the episode, Lucy and Ethel get jobs wrapping chocolates in a candy factory. Their supervisor is tough as nails and shows little or no compassion for the new hires. Using fear motivation to get as much productivity as possible out of Lucy and Ethel, the manipulative supervisor barks the following orders: "All right, girls, if one candy gets past you on this conveyor belt and into the packing room unwrapped—you're fired!"

Motivated by fear that they will lose their jobs, Lucy and Ethel panic when the conveyer belt starts moving faster than they can wrap. Then, when they hear their supervisor approaching, they resort to drastic measures. The rest is comedy history as Lucy and Ethel begin stuffing the unwrapped chocolates down their uniforms and into their mouths.

Because it's Lucy and Ethel, it's funny. But it's not funny at all that there are still supervisors out there who believe that fear will motivate their workers to perform better, when just the opposite is true.

Start by letting employees know that everyone is an equal and important part of the team and, most of all, that everyone is an individual and will be respected as such. Stress that this is a team where everyone is welcome, not a place that rejects people or makes them feel that they don't belong.

Next, emphasize that there are no wrong answers or right ways to achieve the end result. Stress that you are open to new ways of doing things and that it's OK when people don't know the answers, that they should just ask. Another way to keep people from feeling vulnerable and weak is to encourage them to be human and admit their mistakes. No one's perfect—and when someone messes up, everyone learns something. When managers share their past mistakes with employees, they are seen as human and helpful.

Finally, tell employees that individual performance is measured in many ways and that each person will know what is expected of him or her before beginning work. Calm fears by letting employees know that at no time will anyone be set up to feel small or inferior. Remind everyone that you're there to help

all employees build their strengths and improve on their weaknesses.

Dreaded Performance Reviews

Dr. W. Edwards Deming, founder of the quality movement, says
it best: "In practice, annual ratings are a disease, annihilating
long-term planning, demolishing teamwork, nourishing rivalry
and politics, leaving people bitter, crushed, battered, desolate,
despondent, unfit for work for weeks after receipt of rating, and
unable to comprehend why they are inferior." Wow, talk about
your negativity invaders!

But wait! Before you go throwing out the forms for your next
scheduled performance review, stop and consider what could be
a better alternative or a spin to improve what you're using now.
Not all performance reviews are bad. Some can actually be a
valuable source of corrective and positive feedback for employees. The good ones can help employees measure their progress
and establish with managers criteria for ongoing expectations
and goals.

But here's where negativity works its way in. Most performance reviews are not used in a constructive and helpful way. In
fact, they can be quite traumatic, even devastating, if used like
a report card to sum up an employee's contributions and objec-
tify him or her.

Here's an example:
"Well, Marge, when it
comes to being multi-task
oriented, on a scale of one
to five, I've given you a
three, so there's lots of
room for improvement but
you're still doing much
better than most in the
department. Keep trying."
Is it any wonder that Marge
leaves her review feeling

> **No Numbers!** **CAUTION!**
> Never assign numbers
> to people as a way to
> rate their performance. It's humiliating
> and degrading. It only serves to per-
> sonalize that person's weaknesses,
> instead of focusing on the issues.
> Besides, how can a behavior trait be
> changed through a scoring process? It
> can't. It's the organization's system
> that produces its behaviors. Change
> the system and the behaviors will
> change as well.

> ## Don't Let Numbers Create Negative Feelings
>
> If you must use numbers to evaluate performance, then use them to show percentage growth in a specific skill area, such as writing or listening. But even then, percentages should be assigned by the employee, not by the manager. You'd be surprised at how much harder employees can be on themselves than their managers.

humiliated and demoralized? How does Marge explain to her family that she's only a three on a scale of five when it comes to being capable of multi-tasking? The situation is grim.

Your Job Is to Lead, Not Judge

Do you think you're the only manager or supervisor who dreads conducting employee performance reviews? Hah! Most managers and supervisors say they can do without the jockeying required to prepare themselves for the upcoming, possibly painful assessments and nerve-wracking anticipation of each employee's agonizing reaction!

One manager shares his story of performance reviews and why he quit using them.

When I was coming up through the ranks at another firm, during one of my six-month evaluations, my supervisor ranked me satisfactory in one of my key performance areas. As I recall, I was given a number three on some inane scale from one to five. The review devastated me. Not only did it squash my confidence, but it took the air out of my sails and put the kibosh on my can-do attitude. I eventually quit because of it.

Today, I'm a manager in an insurance company and I never use performance appraisals of any kind. Instead, I've come up with more creative ways to help build my employees' talents and give them the necessary and helpful feedback they need to set goals and succeed here. Traditional reviews isn't one of them. I want to be a leader, not a judge."

What can a manager do?

You can start by understanding the real objective of measuring employee performance. It's not to get workers to try and become number one. Rather, the objective should be to encourage workers to want to continually improve themselves, sharpen their talents, and become lifelong learners. A manager who relies solely on evaluating performance using the traditional performance appraisal methods is missing the point. The key is to develop people to their greatest potential using innovative techniques and reevaluating old ones.

One way to make a change for the better is to start *building* employee performance, rather than merely *appraising* it.

To start, focus on how to enhance and build employee performance, confidence, communications skills, vision, understanding, and accountability. Here are seven steps to developing highly effective performers without using a traditional performance appraisal. You'll probably want to adapt the following format to meet your individual management style and the needs of the organization. You can even blend together your present employee evaluation tool and this more flexible, less formal process, adding and deleting to develop something that works best for you.

> **Better Performance Means Higher Morale** TRICKS OF THE TRADE
>
> The objective of switching from a more traditional employee evaluation tool to a performance-enhancing process is to be able to more effectively fight the negativity invaders that lower employee morale. By making the switch, you'll be helping employees reach their peak levels of productivity and individual excellence.

Seven Steps to Building Highly Effective Performers

Step 1. Define what performance means. Never assume that your employees will understand or know what it is you mean by "performance." Define the term based on the circumstances of your organization. It can take on a different meaning depending on whether you're in manufacturing, computers, marketing, travel, or retail.

Avoid Failure and Prepare for Success

If you involve employees in the development of their own performance standards, they'll be more likely to openly discuss with you any obstacles they perceive as getting in the way of their success. Research shows time and again that when employees are involved in measuring their performance, they are more likely to accept and meet the challenge of their managers.

Next, establish with each employee clear and specific performance expectations. Invite your employee to discuss his or her own parameters for measuring performance. This will tell you what the employee believes is realistic.

Step 2. Stretch employees and get buy-in on improving performance. Getting employee buy-in isn't about being manipulative. Employees want to buy into standards of excellence that are truly worthy of their time and energy. Performance building is a joint venture between managers and their employees. It's a partnership. When this happens, employees are far more likely to be willing to stretch themselves to reach higher performance levels.

Step 3. Be clear about the scope of responsibility you are giving. Be explicit. Ask if your employee understands who exactly is responsible for what. When employees understand their responsibilities in relationship to everyone else, the possibility of confusion is quickly reduced or even eliminated.

Step 4. Don't just document what's agreed on—create a course of action! Make a detailed, written list of all the performance standards you and your employee have agreed on. But that's still not enough to ensure success. Now you must be specific about what it's going to take to reach these expectations.

For example, let's say Sarah must be able to handle all of the budgeting requirements for her department to be successful, but math is not her strong suit. You know that Sarah is capable of handling the levels of performance you require, but she just needs a nudge in the right direction. Therefore, Sarah might consider taking an employee budgeting class through the organization's corporate university or at a local community college. To continue her growth, Sarah may want to follow up with introductory management courses and advanced math skills as well to better prepare for future opportunities and promotions within the department. Each requires a step-by-step, specific action.

Plan to Be Spontaneous!

Smart Managing

Help your employees plan to be spontaneous. This may seem like a paradox—because it is. Explain that the scope of responsibility may change at any moment, depending on unforeseen circumstances, and that planning is key. Tell them that adapting to unplanned scenarios is part of the job and that, when this happens, it's perfectly OK to broaden the scope of responsibility. But again, be clear here as to what "broaden the scope of responsibility" means to you. Leave no room for guesswork.

Document all of the action steps that Sarah agrees to take and call this Sarah's "course of action." Give a copy of this document to Sarah and keep one for your file. At the next review, this document will serve as the platform for measuring progress toward the agreed-upon standards of performance.

Step 5. Watch what people are doing and respond. Don't wait a few months or until the next scheduled review with your employee to check up on things. Observe and give feedback to employees while the job's in progress. This sends out a strong message that you're there to help and be supportive.

Step 6. Be specific about what can be expected when goals are met. Let every employee know what's in it for him or her for meeting or exceeding expectations and goals set forth in his or her course of

Warning! Don't Ignore the Obvious

CAUTION!

Pay attention. Keep your eyes open and observe what's going on around you at all times. You don't have to wait for a review to do that. Observation remains one of the best and least expensive measurement tools a manager can use.

action plan. Build in lots of small wins along the way and make recognition part of the system. When you do this, you'll be connecting rewards with behavior. List in the performance builder what specific rewards will be included, such as money, award certificate, a week off, two-hour lunch, letter from the CEO, more responsibility, etc.

Step 7. Give people what they need to make smart moves, then help plan their careers! When it comes to performance building techniques, employee development should be at the top of the list. Think training. Ask employees what they need to learn in order to succeed. Don't just decide for them. Get them what they need, when they need it. Help plan their careers and give them the guidance and resources necessary to make smart moves and decisions.

Deliver Training Ahead of Time

Smart Managing One of the secrets to IBM's earlier success was that the organization gave its people lots and lots of training. They were always thinking ahead. Training is critical, but it has to be timely too. It used to be acceptable to deliver employee development "just in time," but that doesn't cut it any longer. Today managers need to provide employee training ahead of time, not just as close as possible to the time it's needed. In today's cyber-fast world, "close" is not good enough.

Cynical Attitudes

It's no secret that negative attitudes and poor behavior in the workplace are deadly. Costing corporations billions of dollars a year in lowered productivity and weakened performance, negative attitudes and lousy behaviors cannot be ignored. Cynical attitudes and negativity are like contagious diseases that, if left untreated, can spread throughout the organization, affecting even the most upbeat employees and bringing down morale in a hurry.

Managers and supervisors can't be responsible for protecting every employee against negative experiences, but they can certainly help to minimize the overall effects of negative workplace behaviors by taking specific actions to eliminate some of

the deadliest and most common de-motivators that contribute
to low morale and cynical attitudes on the job, which ultimately
eat away at company profits and employee stamina.

So how's it done? Learn from some of the following organizations and their leadership's proven strategies for knocking out
cynical attitudes and replacing them with can-do, never-say-die
work ethics and superstar workplace behaviors.

Here are some examples ....

For one major retailer, superstar behaviors and women rule! At
a major East Coast retail outlet, turnover and poor attitudes
were at an all-time high. More than 40% of its almost all-male
sales team were leaving the company within six months and
bad attitudes were running rampant. The retail chain, on the
verge of expansion, knew it would need to hire more salespeo-
ple in a hurry, but it wanted top performers who would stay with
the company and would help to boost morale, not wreck it.

The solution? The famous retailer took the time to interview
its handful of top performers and identify the common denomi-
nators among them. In-depth behavioral interviews uncovered
the core competencies necessary for doing a super job with an
undying, can-do attitude. Those competencies included things
like high energy, enthusiasm, assertiveness (not aggressive-
ness), and a sincere desire to serve customers and make them
happy. Results also indicated that women were the ones doing
the best job. When the organization launched its recruiting and
hiring efforts in the Southeast, human resource specialists
specifically hired to the competencies they had uncovered and,
voilà! Women were in the majority of the new hires.

**A worldwide housecleaning service eliminates boredom to
boost morale and improve housekeeper attitudes.** One international housekeeping company was experiencing unprecedented
amounts of employee fatigue, burnout, and boredom. With a
critical eye to how cleaning teams carried out their tasks, management came up with an approach to fight boredom and
burnout and enhance overall productivity.

The solution? The first thing supervisors did was create a system to rotate tasks from house to house, so that housekeepers didn't get bored with the same old routines. Next, supervisors revised workers' schedules, to give them more down time between jobs. One manager even scheduled in "chat times" for housekeepers between their assignments. The results were clear: workers were more refreshed, less fatigued, less bored, happier, and more positive about their work—and in less than a year tenure of housekeepers increased by 30%.

Culture councils keep out the negative and lock in the positive. After a period of low-employee morale and fast-spreading negativism, a nationwide mortgage banking company based in Dallas found the secret to maintaining high employee morale and better attitudes after visiting a competitor's Culture Day event. At the event, which spotlighted the organization's high-spirited and positive culture, managers quickly determined that what their own organization needed was a "culture council" to lead it out of the doldrums and make the workplace exciting and more energetic. They saw firsthand what a culture council could do—lock in the greatest things about their company and keep out the naysayers.

The solution? Managers picked culture council representatives from different divisions and branches of the organization. Council representatives had to meet certain criteria: they had to be top performers in their departments, they had to have at least one innovative or creative idea to boost employee morale, they had to have at least five years' tenure so that they could spread the positive stories and successes of the company's culture, and they had to exemplify an unstoppable positive attitude and behavior that inspires others to be their best.

Just getting selected for the council motivated employees, who considered it quite prestigious. Twelve council members were chosen to serve a two-year stint. This term length was to keep council representation fresh and give others a chance to carry the baton. In the first two years, the culture council was such a success that branches nationwide began implementing their own culture councils. Councils eventually became responsible for all corporate events, hiring practices, and workplace fun!

Managers' Challenge

Every company and industry today is faced with the challenge of achieving competitive advantage through its people. So the challenge for managers is for employees to be happy. Remember: unhappiness is a reflection of behaviors and poor attitudes are a reflection of negativity. Of course, there are also going to be the extreme cases of those who turn to bad choices like drugs or alcohol when they're unhappy with their lives and others who may express their dissatisfaction by stealing from the company or ignoring safety regulations and putting others at risk. Although no manager can give his or her employees everything they want in life, showing appreciation and understanding and com-passion can go a long way in registering high on the employee morale meter.

The best managers get the job done through their people and by helping create a healthy and happy work environment. This chapter has given you a practical and down-to-earth guide to battling the negativism that erodes employee morale. But don't stop here. Ask your employees for their input and ideas for maintaining positive workplace morale and corporate spirit. You might be surprised at their enthusiasm for the chance to make a difference and be heard.

> ### Practice FIDO
> There is great wisdom in knowing when to accept the things and the people that you cannot change. That's when it's smart to practice FIDO—"Forget it and drive on!"—which means, even as the manager, there's only so much you can do to meet the needs of your people. When employee behavior's gotten out of your control and all of your helpfulness has been refused, then it's time to accept what you cannot change, make those tough decisions, and get on with it.

Manager's Checklist for Chapter 5

❏ Morale can be measured just like any other area of your business.

❏ Conducting morale audits is critical to knowing what people are really thinking and feeling about their work.

❏ Employee satisfaction committees are the "morale doctors" of the organization and keep small problems from growing.

❏ The top three negativity invaders are fear, dreaded performance reviews, and cynical attitudes.

❏ Never assign numbers to employees as a way to rate their performance. It's humiliating and personalizes the person's weaknesses.

❏ Managers who use performance-building techniques in lieu of traditional performance appraisal tools get better performance results from their people.

❏ Planning to be spontaneous is important when anything in the workplace can change at the drop of a hat.

❏ Managers must deliver important training to employees ahead of time, not just in time.

❏ Cynical attitudes and sloppy workplace behaviors cost companies billions of dollars in employee productivity and performance.

The High Price of Low Morale: Six Morale Challenges and Six Toolkits

There's a high price to pay for low morale. No, make that an *enormous* price. So, what does it cost an organization when morale hits bottom? Well, what's the cost of turnover, bad attitudes, decreased productivity, low self-esteem, poor performance, absenteeism, and lousy customer service? Oh, yeah, and don't forget the decreased profits and lower return on shareholders' investment.

Basically, there are two prevailing cultures among business leaders. One is a culture of acceptance—acceptance that employees are always going to be disinterested and can be motivated only extrinsically, with more money and benefits and perks. The other is a culture that is fully aware and empathetic to the challenges that managers and employees are facing. It's a culture of business leaders who strongly believe that an organization can achieve greatness only through its people and

Morale and Motivation—Extrinsic and Intrinsic

Smart Managing When employees are *extrinsically* motivated, it means that they're looking for things outside of themselves that will influence their behavior to perform at their peak. Extrinsic motivators are found in incentives like promotions, raises, bonuses, rewards, and other expensive perks. The impact of these extrinsic motivators on morale can be short-lived.

When employees are *intrinsically* motivated, it means they're moved to take action by something deeper, something within that fulfills them in some way. *Intrinsic* motivation has greater impact on morale than *extrinsic* motivation in the long run.

only when those people are motivated intrinsically, when they find meaning and a sense of purpose in their work, desire to accomplish something worthwhile, and love their jobs. These are the managers for whom this book was written.

Solutions for the Six Most Common Morale Problems

You may find yourself referencing this chapter again and again more than any other chapter in this book. Why? Because this chapter addresses real workplace scenarios and recommends specific things you can do as a manager when employee morale is threatened or tumbling. Think of this chapter as your personal toolkit, with fast solutions, easy-to-use tips and techniques, and possible answers for handling some of the most common morale busters.

How to Make This Chapter Work for You

This chapter presents six scenarios of the most common on-the-job performance and morale problems. First, read the Manager's Morale Challenge. Then, before doing anything else, think about how you might handle the situation in your own organization or how well you've dealt with similar situations in the past. Make notes. Next, compare your solutions with the solutions and techniques offered in the Manager's Toolkit section of the scenario. By combining your experiences managing people and the recommendations offered here, you'll have some effective ways to handle these most common performance issues and morale problems.

Of course there are no absolute "right" ways to handle a morale-threatening situation. Every manager must use his or her judgment based on the organization, the people involved, and other factors

> ### Take Notes
>
> Smart Managing
>
> As you encounter performance scenarios on the job that directly impact company morale, take notes and start preparing your own addendum to the Manager's Toolkit. Ask other managers and supervisors for their input as well. Before you know it, you'll have compiled a valuable resource from which future managers and supervisors will learn and benefit.

specific to the situation. However, it's always good to know that you have a place to turn when the going gets particularly rough. That place is this chapter, where you'll find suggestions and ideas for making your job a little easier.

Manager's Morale Challenge #1: Rumors

In any community of people, rumors are inevitable. People circulate rumors because they're concerned, worried, curious, bored, or mean. In the workplace, rumors can affect morale both positively and negatively—usually negatively.

How serious do rumors have to become before they affect employee morale? When does a manager need to get involved? That depends. Managers know that rumors in the workplace are inevitable. But if the rumor mill is working at full capacity and rumors start flying that instill fear or malice in the hearts of your employees, then you've got a real problem that you must address on the double.

Managers often choose to simply ignore the rumors they know to be untrue and to concentrate on the tales that have merit but are distorted to the point that they constitute a serious threat to employee morale. However, you should also consider the scope of the rumors. If the rumors affect everyone and seem to have developed out of a general concern, you can sim-

Rumors: Step in or Stay out?

When is a rumor serious enough that you should inter-
vene? When is it just a bit of harmless gossip that you can
safely ignore? Let's consider two examples.

You hear through the grapevine that Matt is interviewing for a position with Company X. That rumor probably has some merit and you
can decide whether or not it's worth approaching Matt about it. It's
relevant only if you want it to be. It directly involves just Matt and you;
the other employees are merely interested bystanders.

Downsizing is a real possibility in your department, but there are
no decisions yet and no specific plans. If rumors are running rampant
that half of your employees are going to lose their jobs without severance pay or even two weeks' notice, then you can expect pandemoni-
um and panic, which threatens morale. That's a rumor mill any manager needs to stop immediately.

ply bring them up at a meeting and put them to rest. But when
there are specific perpetrators and/or specific victims, you
should take action immediately and prudently. If a manager
doesn't act to dispel rumors, employees victimized by the
rumors may take legal action.

Start using some of the following techniques when putting
the kibosh on harmful rumors.

Manager's Toolkit

- In virtually every organization, people want to know
  what's going on. If they don't get the information they
  want from management soon enough, they will find other
  means (usually rumors) to do so. So get information to
  your employees fast and frequently.
- As a manager, you will more than likely be removed from
  the rumor mill. This makes it all the more important for
  you to keep your eyes open and your ear to the ground at
  all times. Don't be the last to know.
- Take the initiative. Ask your employees what they want to
  know and then tell them before any rumors start.
- Minimize the damage. Go to your employees first before
  going to outside sources to verify information they've

heard elsewhere. Explore how rumors are directly impacting employee morale and then focus your energies in those areas.

- Take what you hear seriously, but don't react until you know all the facts. Think about how you will respond before you actually do.
- Campaign against spreading rumors with wit. Post on your door, bulletin boards, or wherever a few quotes such as the following:
  - "Gossip is sometimes referred to as halitosis of the mind." —Unknown
  - "Who gossips to you will gossip about you." —Proverb
  - "Conversation is an exercise of the mind; gossip is merely an exercise of the tongue." —Unknown
  - "The things most people want to know about are usually none of their business." —George Bernard Shaw
  - "You can tell more about a person by what he says about others than you can by what others say about him." —Leo Aikman
- Use rumors as a way to develop a keener sense about what you need to do to be a better manager.
- If you get wind of a rumor you know to be incorrect, correct it immediately and support your information with facts. If you don't know the facts, get them.
- Use the rumor mill. Occasionally you might want to float your own messages

> **CAUTION!**
>
> **Two Rules for Handling Rumors**
>
> 1. Almost all rumors have some piece of truth associated with them, however small.
> 2. If a rumor is repeated, you can bet there's an issue that the people are talking about and care about. Don't ignore it.

through the mill. For example, you may wish to send a strong and forceful message that certain employee behaviors won't be tolerated, like carelessness about safety, lying, drinking on the job, or sexual harassment.

Tricks of the Trade

Use the Rumor Mill

Plenty of experienced managers have used the rumor mill for their own benefit. Managers sometimes go so far as to leak a message regarding new policies, unacceptable employee behaviors, upcoming announcements, or impending changes. After all, business moguls, politicians, and celebrities have been successfully using this tactic with the media for years as a way of influencing public opinion.

Manager's Morale Challenge #2: Resistance to Change and Authority

People tend to resist change, especially in the workplace. They may not understand what the changes entail, they may disagree with the reasons for making the changes, they may not appreciate the benefits, they may be afraid of losing something they value, they may be concerned that they won't have the skills and ability to handle the changes …. Many people also tend to resist authority, for various reasons. Resistance can do serious damage to morale, dividing employees and causing frustration, resentment, and distrust.

You're trying to make some changes to improve the way your unit works. All of your employees are accepting the changes, more or less—except two people. Those individuals are resisting, questioning the changes, complaining about them. Their resistance is beginning to disrupt the unit and affect morale. What should you do?

You've worked darn hard to develop an environment that encourages honest and open feedback, so now's the time to use it. Whatever you do, don't avoid the problem just because the two employees are performing adequately. If they're negatively affecting morale, then it's time to take charge and get things out on the table. Invite the resisters to offer their input to you in private. Take the approach that the information you will receive may transform into positive results for everyone involved.

Try the following ways to handle employees who are negatively resisting the changes you're attempting to initiate.

Manager's Toolkit

- Deal with the issues head on. If you don't deal openly and honestly with resistance to change and authority, it will build and cause more serious morale issues down the line. By addressing the issues head on, you can avoid possible sabotage or much tougher employee problems.
- Keep in mind that someone who's resisting change and authority may be simply expressing negative energy that could have nothing to do with you personally or with the organization.
- Take time to probe and to better understand your employee's viewpoint and feelings about the matter. Try to uncover the real reasons for resisting management's decisions and the changes taking place. It might not be as obvious as you think. Ask, "What's really behind this, John?" "Is there more to this than you're telling me?" "What's the real problem you're having, Lou?"
- Share your perceptions of these same issues as well. Managers manage perceptions. They don't let the perceptions manage them.
- Let the employee know that you appreciate his or her feelings and are trying to understand them.
- Listen carefully and answer any questions. If you don't know the answers, find out. Try to find a way to work with this person more comfortably. Focus on the person's individual objectives and desires, not his or her personality.
- Never argue with an employee or attempt to sell your viewpoint. Just explain it from the heart. Let the employee know specifically how his or her actions and negative behaviors are making you feel. Don't get defensive.
- Acknowledge and validate concerns expressed by the employee. Remember: most people are seeking acknowledgment of their feelings and opinions more than anything else.
- Deal with only one issue at a time. Address it and then move on to the next point.

- Be patient. The time and energy that you invest in resolving the problem will likely pay off big-time in terms of morale.
- Summarize the employee's point of view to ensure that you have understood everything correctly. If not, ask for clarification and then summarize your understanding again.
- Ask for support. As manager, you have the right to ask that your employees not tear down the morale of others or deliberately block your efforts when you're making every attempt to do your job to the best of your ability. Point out how this resistance is affecting others. Be specific. Offer examples. The person may not even realize the power of his or her negativity.
- Let your employee know exactly what you expect. Ask how you can offer support and help facilitate his or her success in the organization. Ask what he or she needs in order to stop bucking authority and start accepting the changes. Make it clear that this individual's approval of the changes is not required.
- Ask what might be standing in the way of a mutual and positive working arrangement that boosts everyone's morale and supports the team. Encourage questions and be open to new ideas and opinions. Don't expect this type of situation to be easy. But it should not be impossible.

Manager's Morale Challenge #3: Whiners and Chronic Complainers

Some people seem to find fault with just about everything. These people can be valuable when you need some critical thinking about an idea or an issue, but otherwise they can annoy their fellow employees, get on your nerves, and undermine morale.

The first step to take when dealing with whiners and complainers is to start by understanding the four basic reasons why employees whine or complain:

1. They want attention.
2. They want you to solve their problems for them.
3. They seek nurturing from a parental figure.
4. They have a need to be heard.

Once you understand these four basic reasons why people complain, you can begin to address the problem more effectively. But remember this. Performance and productivity are the primary issues that should concern you as a manager. It's not your responsibility to make people feel good all of the time, nor is it your duty to ensure their constant happiness. Employees are just as responsible for their own happiness and morale. Accountability is key here. Ask yourself, "Is the environment contributing to the constant complaining?" If the answer is yes, you may be in luck, because then there's a good chance you can change things.

Check out your toolkit for possible ideas and solutions when dealing with chronic complainers.

Manager's Toolkit

- Start by being an empathetic listener.
- Treat complainers and whiners like adults, not children. Let them know you have confidence in their ability to handle a variety of situations with positive results.
- If the complaining has no bearing on productivity,

Six Fast Ways to Handle Complainers

1. Listen carefully and paraphrase.
2. Examine the *context*, not the *content*, of the complaint.
3. Clarify the complaint. That doesn't mean you're agreeing with the complainer, but indicates that you're paying close attention.
4. Analyze the facts in preparation for a solution.
5. Determine whether or not the complaint has a direct impact on immediate or long-term productivity and overall morale of the team.
6. Invite employees to offer their own solutions.

then simply listen, but don't necessarily attempt to make the situation better.

- Here are some helpful questions you might want to ask during the discussion:
  - "What options do you have?"
  - "What are you specifically asking for in this situation?"
  - "Are you open to other solutions?"
  - "I'm really interested in what you have to say. Can you tell me more?"
  - "How do you plan to solve this?"
- Finally, let the employee know that you intend to monitor the situation, especially the impact on morale among employees. Explain the importance of creating a high-morale work environment and the energy drain that takes place every time someone complains without offering a viable solution to the problem. Put the complainer in the shoes of others who are being affected negatively. Arrange to follow up at a specific time and date.

Manager's Morale Challenge #4: Personal Problems

We all have personal problems. Generally we can leave them behind when we come to work or at least get our minds off them enough to do our jobs. But sometimes our personal problems affect our performance and even hurt morale.

Before you became a manager, you probably never imagined how involved you would become in your employees' personal problems. But by now you know that's part of the job. However, lots of managers, maybe you're one of them, feel very uncomfortable when it comes to any kind of personal counseling of employees. But you know you've got to do something when you sense that an employee's personal problems are affecting his or her job performance and morale.

Try putting to use some of these tips in your toolkit for delicately uncovering personal issues that are bringing down morale.

Manager's Toolkit

- Start the conversation with your own personal observations. Perhaps there's been a change in the employee's performance that makes you wonder if there's a problem. For example, if an employee is always punctual and then begins arriving late for work without calling or offering an explanation, this would be an indication of a pattern gone off track. Employees don't just suddenly change their behaviors without a reason. But don't jump to conclusions. Show concern, not anger.

- Equip yourself when getting ready to talk with an employee about impaired performance or lack of morale. It's likely that personal issues will arise. Be knowledgeable and prepared to offer information about your organization's Employee Assistance Program (EAP) and any other valuable resources that might be available. The more resources you can suggest to a troubled employee, the more likely he or she is to pursue one of those options. Provide suggestions, names, addresses, phone numbers, and Web sites *in writing*. Don't expect a worried employee to remember all of your suggestions from your meeting.

- Personal matters are a very delicate area. Even the most seasoned managers should never pry too deeply, accuse, or judge. You can demonstrate genuine concern without delving too far into someone's personal life. You're there to be supportive, not a psychiatrist.

Private Property: Keep Out   **⚠ CAUTION!**

Never discuss personal issues unless the employee volunteers them. Don't ask about anything personal; stick to behavior on the job. If an employee has been absent a lot lately, for example, you may talk about the effects on performance and morale. Then, if the employee confides that it's because he's been taking his wife to chemotherapy treatments, you may then offer to help him with resources and time off. Let the employee bring up personal issues. If that doesn't happen, don't pry.

- Be clear and upfront about your objectives for meeting with this employee and your desire to help no matter what the problem. Reiterate your expectations for performance. Explain that you're depending on this employee to get the job done. Also explain your concern about the effects of poor performance on the team and their morale. Try to resist becoming entangled in your employee's personal life. However, that should not keep you from being compassionate, understanding, and genuinely concerned for the well-being of your employee.

- Help uncover options. Examine the possibilities and choices available, depending on the problem. Effectively coach your employee to help him or her make a decision, but don't tell your employee what to do or how to do it.

- At some point you'll have to discuss the consequences if the performance problem continues or if the employee refuses help. Be honest and direct about the matter.

- Provide your employee with every opportunity to save face and bounce back successfully. That's what great managers do best: they help their people succeed.

- Always protect the confidentiality and privacy of your employees. Never repeat something about an employee's personal life without his or her permission to do so. Your credibility as a manager is on the line.

- Finally, set a time to meet again and review the corrective actions that the two of you have agreed on. That might include a leave of absence, a long weekend, a transfer

What to Do if an Employee Refuses Help

Smart Managing If an employee doesn't respond to your suggestions for assistance, do not make threats a part of the discussion. The objective is to clear the air and solve the performance problem together. Help your employee to reconsider. Explain again the demands of the job and how his or her behavior affects other people. Discuss whether or not the job is still a good fit and then explore other options available to the employee. Never offer solutions or options that you're not willing or able to provide or support.

to another department, or counseling with a professional. Place the responsibility on the employee to make the changes you've discussed. Continue to offer your support and monitor performance progress just as you would for any other performance improvement goal.

Manager's Morale Challenge #5: Defensive Attitudes

Many of us get defensive from time to time. In fact, the problem may be growing. (We've certainly seen an increase in road rage, which shows how quickly some people can react defensively—and take it to extremes.) But sometimes being defensive is more than just a reaction to a certain situation. If it's an attitude that makes an employee generally jumpy or bristly, it's definitely going to chip away at morale.

What's a manager to do with an employee who's got a defensive attitude? There's certainly nothing more pervasive than the attitude of a person who spreads negativity or puts down everyone and everything the team is trying to accomplish. This can be a manager's greatest challenge—communicating effectively with an employee who constantly reacts defensively on the job.

Attitude is everything, so pay close attention to the tips in your toolkit and some of the ways you may be able to better handle defensive attitudes and protect morale.

Manager's Toolkit

- Start by evaluating yourself. Is there any specific reason why people might be misinterpreting or misreading you? Ask yourself, "Is it what I'm saying or the way I'm saying it that may be provoking this response from the people I manage? Have I been sarcastic or unintentionally curt or abrupt with people who need my help? Am I causing this behavior or is it the person I need to be concerned about?"
- Make an effort to sharpen your own interpersonal skills. Take a class or read some books on the subject. Sign up

Mirror Body Language to Build Rapport

Smart Managing   Body language can be very revealing and effective when trying to build rapport with someone. Use body language to convey that you're comfortable to be with and that you're not on the attack or a threat to anyone. To do this, study the communication style of the employee with whom you're seeking to gain rapport and mirror it to set him or her at ease. For example, if the person's body language is casual and laid back, then try to do the same to create a comfort zone for better communication.

for an online or distance-learning program to improve your communications skills.

- Work on building strong individual relationships. Build rapport with employees by taking a genuine approach to communicating clearly and to listening carefully to what others are really defending. You may be surprised by what you actually hear them saying, compared with what you thought their attitudes were conveying.
- Try to determine where an employee's defensive behavior is coming from. Most people with defensive attitudes are protecting themselves from others who they fear will make them feel or look incompetent or unproductive. This defensive mechanism also comes from a basic lack of self-esteem or insecurity about a person's own power and status.
- Seek to find a common ground with this person.
- Try to convince the employee that you're not an adversary and that you want an enjoyable and mutually respectful and productive relationship. Let the person know that you want to learn and grow from your employees.
- Detach yourself from the attitude and defensive reactions of the person. If you argue or act defensively, you will lose. As the manager, you cannot afford to argue with any of your employees. If you do this, you will lose employee trust and only further weaken the relationship.
- You're the manager, so remain in control at all times. Never become defensive. Stay calm.

- Use "I" statements when discussing a situation with a defensive employee, such as "I'm concerned about something, Mary" or "I asked you about this a few days ago and I have not heard anything on the status of the job."
- Summarize and clarify to the best of your ability any defensive remarks you hear at the time they occur. Ask questions and don't judge. Don't argue.
- Encourage accountability.
- Accept that a person's feelings, even if they seem unfair or ungrounded to you, are real for that person.
- Express clearly that you want to understand the barriers that obviously exist and to work to build an alliance of support and mutual respect. Ask the employee to suggest ways to do so.
- Offer to pay for your employee to take self-confidence or esteem-building training. More and more organizations are offering such training through their corporate universities or making it available through outside seminars and retreats.
- Consider making this issue of improving self-esteem a topic for your next department retreat or staff meeting. Include everyone in the program so that no one is singled out.
- Most of all, as the manager, you have every right to ask for and expect respect. Do it now.

Manager's Morale Challenge #6: Fewer Resources and/or More Demands

It's a tough situation. Maybe the organization has cut staff and budget. Maybe upper management keeps demanding more of you and your employees. Maybe both. A natural consequence is that employees are bound to suffer burnout and become angry and that will affect morale. In fact, morale can be so affected that you worry about getting the work done.

Let's face it—in such circumstances, it's just not a fun place to work anymore. So what's a manager to do? What's the answer to keeping employee morale and performance up when employees are feeling down because of burnout, cutbacks, layoffs, increased demands, and insecurity about the future?

Open up your toolkit for some ways to deal with these situations.

Manager's Toolkit

- When situations are ambiguous, employees want information and plenty of warning of things to come. They also want reasons and explanations. As the manager, you must work harder to gather information from senior management about the future and then inform your staff. Get specifics you can relay. Why were the changes made? What's likely to occur from this point forward?
- Try emphasizing the positive aspects of any major changes that are going to impact your employees, such as how employees will be trained in new technology or how the new branding campaign will make the organization more competitive in the marketplace.
- Listen to your employees. Spend time with them. You don't have to have all the answers; you just have to be available.
- Get people to think forward and move forward. Tell employees to forget the past and the way things used to be. Focus on the here and now. Focus on creating a better tomorrow even with these new constraints.
- Be realistic in setting performance and productivity goals for your people. Discuss what's possible.
- Make it a point to celebrate every success and achievement. Don't shine the light on what didn't get done. Set people up for success, not failure.
- You'll be expecting more from every employee, so you must be willing to give more in return. Tell them so. Try to help your employees find greater meaning and purpose in

their work. Empower them to make critical decisions on their own. Ask every employee to take more responsibility for solving problems and being innovative. Encourage them to take on self-directed and intentional learner attitudes and greater responsibility for their own growth and development.

> **How to Do More with Less**
> *Smart Managing*
>
> When managers are expected to do more with less, they quickly learn how to wisely manage people under adverse conditions. That means helping their employees get more involved and develop their skills, take more responsibility, and become more accountable for their actions. If you're going to demand more from your employees, you have to keep their morale high, show that you appreciate them, and give them the power to take action and make a significant difference on their own.

- Take time to discuss with people on a regular basis all of the changes taking place. Let everyone know that you're going to be building a new kind of team and that everyone is in this together. If the team is to survive and thrive under difficult circumstances, then the members will have to do it together.
- If you want to boost morale in tough times, then you must treat all of your employees like partners. Always give them the benefit of the doubt and trust that they will always act in the best interest of the team and the organization, as well as in their own best interests. As with the Pygmalion Effect, expectations will influence behavior.

> **Pygmalion Effect** *Key Term*
>
> The phenomenon in which expectations about a person can eventually lead that person to behave and achieve in ways that confirm those expectations. It's human nature that people will try to meet your expectations of them. In short, high expectations lead to higher performance—and low expectations lead to lower performance. So, you have to communicate *high* expectations and communicate them *clearly*.

Pygmalion and Morale

Smart Managing   "What managers believe about themselves subtly influences what they believe about their subordinates, what they expect of them, and how they treat them. If they have confidence in their ability to develop and stimulate them to high levels of performance, they will expect much of them and will treat them with confidence that their expectations will be met. But if they have doubts about their ability to stimulate them, they will expect less of them and will treat them with less confidence."—J. Sterling Livingston, author of "Pygmalion in Management" (*Harvard Business Review*, July-August 1969). Not bad advice for any manager faced with challenging times and impossible demands. Save this quote and review it regularly.

Develop Your Tactics for Addressing Morale Challenges

The six Manager's Morale Challenges presented in this chapter were selected because they represent some of the most common and challenging scenarios for managers and their struggle to maintain a high level of employee morale.

As a manager, you should use your experience, your unique abilities, and your knowledge of your employees, the culture of your workplace, and the structure of your organization to go beyond the general recommendations offered here. By studying and practicing various ways of addressing a challenge, you will be prepared to better handle performance issues and, more important, not let them destroy the morale you've worked so hard to promote.

Manager's Checklist for Chapter 6

❑ There are two prevailing cultures among business leaders. One believes that employees are motivated only extrinsically and the other believes that an organization can achieve greatness only when its people are motivated intrinsically.

❑ One gauge that managers use to measure the importance of a rumor is to simply ignore the rumors that they know to be untrue and concentrate on the rumors that have merit and could possibly trigger serious morale problems.

❏ Never argue with an employee or attempt to sell your viewpoint. Just explain it from the heart. Let the employee know specifically how his or her actions and negative behavior are making you feel and how they are affecting the morale of the workplace.

❏ Treat employees who are complainers and whiners like adults, not children. Let them know you have confidence in their ability to handle a variety of situations with positive results.

❏ At some point you will have to discuss the consequences if an employee continues to perform poorly or refuses help. Be honest and direct about the matter.

❏ Always protect the confidentiality and privacy of your employees. Never repeat something about an employee's personal life without his or her permission to do so.

❏ Seek to find common ground with employees who are defensive.

❏ Whether the problem affecting morale is burnout, cutbacks, or layoffs, listen to your employees. Spend time with them. You don't have to have all the answers; you just have to be available.

❏ If you intend to build positive morale among employees, start by treating them all like partners.

Hard-Core
Morale Cases

You know the saying—"There are two sides to every story." Well, there are two sides to every supposed dead-end job or hard-core morale case, too. What makes it so tough for one employee to experience any enthusiasm for a so-called "less desirable" job and yet another employee, in an almost identical job but working in a different atmosphere for a different manager, actually loves his or her work and manages to be enthusiastic day in and day out?

While I conducted dozens of interviews for this chapter, the answer kept coming back to one common denominator—it's all in the way managers treat their people. And let's face it: some managers are the problem. They end up creating a low morale atmosphere simply because they hold certain positions in lesser regard and convey that attitude to the ranks, an attitude that's bound to rub off on the people and dilute enthusiasm over time.

Managers Who Get It

And then there are those managers who just seem to get it. They figure out creative ways to bolster morale for every position they supervise. They instill a sense of meaning and value for each person at every level, not just the top dogs. These managers appreciate that a job might seem less desirable to one person but would interest another, who may want to take it on and could be happy and satisfied doing it well. These same managers realize that every worker defines his or her level of success differently and they respect those differences. They acknowledge that not everyone wants to be in a position of greater responsibility. Some employees like what they're doing, no matter how tough the job or conditions, and they take great pride in doing it to the best of their ability. But an awful lot hinges on whether or not that person feels valued and appreciated by management.

This chapter examines the significant differences a manager can make in building better employee morale in the face of what some may consider the least desirable of jobs or the toughest of morale cases. This chapter answers the questions: Who's doing it right? How do effective managers compensate for some of the more difficult workplace scenarios? And more important, when it comes to creating a high morale workplace, which organizations really get it?

Four Seasons Hotel Gets It!

While on a business trip in Austin, Texas, I stayed at the Four Seasons Hotel. I walked into my room mid-morning to find the room attendant (housekeeper) on her hands and knees scrubbing the bathroom floor. I apologized for catching her off guard and let her know I was just popping in to grab a file. At that moment, she not only turned around to face me, but she stood up to greet me with a big smile. This was a first. How often does a room attendant who's in the middle of scrubbing the bathroom floor stand to greet a guest and then smile warmly to boot? The answer is practically never.

The writer in me said I'd better take advantage of this moment and do a quick interview.

"You're working awfully hard," I said. "What makes you so upbeat?"

Mary, the room attendant, didn't miss a chance to answer. "Each of these rooms is like my own business. This entire floor is my business," she boasted.

"Gee, you act like you own the place," I responded.

"I do," said Mary. What she meant was that she took ownership in her work. Here was a person in a job that many would consider undesirable. It might even be a job where enthusiasm and a positive outlook may be hard to find at some hotels, but not at the Four Seasons.

"There are no undesirable jobs here at the Four Seasons," stresses Ade Saleh, Training Manager for the tony hotel's San Francisco location.

Being a pot washer at this glamorous hotel is far from glamorous work, but it doesn't matter, because pot washers at the Four Seasons know how important they are to the hotel's success. "We don't hesitate to tell our pot washers that they hold one of the most important positions in the hotel," says Saleh. "Workers are quite aware of their value to the organization and therefore express their pride on a daily basis. Think about it. If our pot washers weren't doing their jobs, we'd be out of business. All of our employees are working here because they have an inner desire to be hospitable in whatever position they choose to work in at the hotel."

It doesn't matter if you're a pot washer or an upper-level manager at the Four Seasons Hotels. Every employee at every level is treated with equal respect and trust and, as a result, workers in what might appear to be some of the least desirable jobs in the hotel industry are actually doing what they love to do. How does the hotel ensure this high morale?

"It starts in recruitment," says Saleh. No matter what the job, every job candidate is interviewed by at least four managers at the hotel. "We look for people who meet our very spe-

Macaroni Grill Gets It!

Dishwashers at Macaroni Grill in Sacramento, California maintain high morale, according to managing partner Monica Hamden. Although being a dishwasher might seem ho-hum to some, the Macaroni Grill dishwashers don't feel that way.

"Our back-of-the-house people, like prep cooks and dishwashers, for instance, know that they are my internal customers," says Hamden. "Therefore it is my responsibility to treat all of my internal customers at Macaroni Grill with respect and create an environment that they will enjoy working in."

Monica says that the staple of her management technique is the Golden Rule, which means to treat others as you would want to be treated. She also advises managers to take the time to pen their own personal mission statement for their staff. Here's how Monica's personalized mission statement reads for her team at Macaroni Grill:

"We are a Golden Rule restaurant dedicated to delivering world-class food quality and guest service in an atmosphere of mutual respect, trust, teamwork, and fun."

Finally, Monica credits the foundation and integrity of her effective management philosophies to the best-selling book, *Jesus CEO: Using Ancient Wisdom for Visionary Leadership* by Laurie Beth Jones (New York: Hyperion, 1995).

cific internal criteria of desired characteristics and traits. We also want people who are obsessed with making our guests happy. We want employees to be themselves at all times. This works well because there is mutual respect and trust among everyone here."

The Four Seasons Hotels were named one of *Fortune* magazine's 100 Best Companies to Work For in 2002. The upscale hotel chain also pays its housekeeping staff almost 50% more than the hospitality industry average. In addition, to boost employee morale, workers get free hotel stays and a 50% discount on meals and beverages.

Banking Can Be Tough on Morale

Some of the toughest employee morale cases can be found in the financial world. The tumultuous world of banking suffers

Tips for Creating Enthusiasm in Jobs Tough on Morale

- Create a feeling of belonging.
- Take everyone on a field trip for team building and re-energize their commitment to one another.
- All employees are managers' internal customers; therefore, managers serve their employees, not the other way around.
- Give workers the tools they need to do the job.
- Treat everyone with respect.
- Make eye contact and greet everyone when you first come to work.
- Say "Please" and "Thank you."

Source: Monica Hamden, managing partner of Macaroni Grill in Sacramento, California.

from high turnover and low morale. Every time you turn around, it seems like another bank is merging, acquiring, folding, downsizing, upsizing, or restructuring.

One former executive vice president at one of the nation's leading banking institutions in Charlotte, North Carolina—we'll call him Mark—puts it this way:

> Banking has traditionally been very bureaucratic when it comes to making people feel valued. High morale was never a priority when I was in the industry. Top leadership at our bank handed down mandates and in turn that made people at all levels below that feel small and insignificant. Tellers, loan officers, and other frontline workers took the brunt of customer dissatisfaction on a daily basis and then got little or no support from the organization.
>
> Leadership committees rolled out strategic plans promising to change things and never even asked for feedback from the people who actually were doing the jobs. When this happened, it killed morale big time. To our frontline employees, every memo was just another meaningless directive imposed from the top, a lot of empty strategies created by top brass in ivory towers who had nothing to do with day-to-day banking reality and

who could care less about the people in the trenches. People at our bank felt very uncared for and their self-worth was pretty low. These were the toughest employee morale cases I ever had to handle and frankly I didn't handle them well because I didn't have the tools or support to change things.

One idea I had was to create a formal employee development program that prepared people for succession opportunities. I knew if we could offer something like this to our people they would see that we were taking an interest in them and their future. Unfortunately, the suggestion was never given the green light and that's when I resigned.

Despite the challenge in today's banking environment, there are some banks out there with progressive and responsive leaders who are doing it right—like at the Bank of Montreal.

Bank of Montreal Gets It!

You might say that the Bank of Montreal is an atypical financial institution. In a world of initiatives focused on the bottom line, Bank of Montreal's culture is all about innovation and people.

Bank of Montreal is known for recognizing that employees are the most important part of its future. The bank states that their people, at all levels within the organization, are both partners and facilitators of their success and that all employees are encouraged to develop a sense of proprietorship in their work. That sense of ownership is evidenced throughout the ranks by consistently high employee morale.

According to one of the bank's financial services managers, "Bank of Montreal is strongly involved in continuing education with their employees." The financial institution has long been committed to serving customers in a dynamic workplace of high employee morale where managers are committed to training and lifelong learning for their workers and ongoing career development is a big part of that.

Bank of Montreal is a respected leader in encouraging

Corporate Values Drive Morale and Keep It High

A Bank of Montreal telebanking manager says, "At the Bank, all positions are guided by the same principles." The bank is built upon and driven by powerful values, which results in high morale.

Bank of Montreal's Values

- We care about our customers, shareholders, communities and each other.
- We draw our strength from the diversity of our people and our businesses.
- We insist upon respect for everyone and encourage all to have a voice.
- We keep our promises and stand accountable for our every action.
- We share information, learn and innovate to create consistently superior customer experiences.

essential career development within the organization. Under its HR umbrella, the Career Center offers employees access to the bank's Possibilities Center. That name alone sums up the organization's unique approach to growing and developing people to reach their full potential. The Center is used as a main resource in preparing both future and present employees for a wide array of career opportunities.

The Career Center at Bank of Montreal offers helpful tools and tips on interviewing techniques, professional networking, résumé writing, and a student career library where future financial professionals can gain access to information about new graduate opportunities with the bank and other helpful career guidance.

You might be thinking, "That's fine for smaller banking institutions, but it's tougher to maintain high employee morale in the big leagues." Well, Bank of Montreal *is* the big leagues. It's one of the largest banks in Canada and North America, with over $246 billion (Canadian) in assets and more than 33,000 employees around the world. While other financial institutions are battling their internal demons in a struggle to build employee morale, take notice, because Bank of Montreal is doing it right!

> ### Commitment to Values Helped UPS Take on Its Toughest Morale Challenge
> **Smart Managing**
>
> In 1997, United Parcel Service (UPS) experienced a gut-wrenching and traumatic drivers' strike, crippling morale and negatively affecting customer opinion worldwide. To restore employee morale and pride, UPS reinvented itself by recommitting to some old and some new cultural values that would ultimately make both its employees and its customers excited about the company. The values included increased reliability, efficiency, procedural uniformity, and higher standards in customer service. The result? Net income for the delivery organization doubled—and so did workers' morale.

Law Enforcement—Saving Lives Saves Morale

Read the headlines: "Police calls up—domestic violence on the rise," "Precinct morale plummets," "Police morale at all-time low following school shooting." It's no secret that law enforcement is notorious for officer morale problems. And that's understandable when, for example, it can be difficult to measure the success of fighting crime or making a direct impact on a specific crime, like domestic violence or guns in schools.

Like many organizations, law enforcement agencies look for ways to measure success and demonstrate to the community that action has produced positive results. When this happens, employee morale is directly affected in a positive way.

Charleston Police Department Gets It!

The police department in Charleston, South Carolina, is one example of how law enforcement develops ways to provide vital morale-building feedback to both its officers and the community.

The department uses city statistics as a weapon to develop better crime-fighting programs that can result in encouraging and motivating feedback for their officers, as well as the community they serve.

For example, soaring numbers on domestic violence made police realize that they needed to make a drastic change in arrest procedures. Charleston's Police Department focused on developing a severe and effective program that would actually deter offenders. The objective was to save lives and avoid the usual arrest-and-release scenario that only contributes to low morale for everyone and lack of faith in the system.

The innovative police department came up with a program that places the spotlight on public arrests for domestic violence. To show they mean business, officers go to workplaces to make arrests, rather than going to homes.

As one local physician found out, when it comes to domestic violence, the Charleston police don't fool around. After being charged with beating his wife, the doctor was arrested in his own waiting room in front of all his patients and staff. An effective and measurable deterrent to domestic violence? You bet. An effective way to tell police and victims that they're making a difference? Absolutely. Soon after the program was implemented, additional statistics gave police in Charleston just what they were hoping for—fewer women were dying of physical abuse following the powerful display of enforcement using the public arrest program.

"This can be a very difficult profession when it comes to keeping morale up," says one law enforcement official who

---

Kids, Guns, and Morale

TRICKS OF THE TRADE

Charleston police gathered crucial statistics on kids and guns in Charleston city schools and the numbers were on the rise. The stats gave police just what they needed to come up with an effective program called Gun Stoppers. The objective of the program is to take away the glory and prestige that kids get from carry guns. Knowing that most kids bring weapons to school to show off, the Charleston police set out to burst that popularity bubble.

The police give $100 the same day to any person who tells police that someone in school has a gun and where that gun is—whether it's in a student's locker, on the playground, in a desk, or a backpack. And the reward applies to toy guns too.

Morale among school officials and officers greatly improved when they received feedback that the program was working. Right after implementing Gun Stoppers, there were no guns found in any of Charleston's city schools.

Compressed Work Schedules Bolster LAPD Morale

Officer morale within the Los Angeles Police Department (LAPD) was dangerously low. A USC/UCLA survey reported in October 2000 that 57% of officers would leave the department if they had a chance. And in 2000, over 300 officers resigned from the LAPD for a variety of reasons, the highest number in years.

That's when the LAPD decided to address the root of the problem—low officer morale.

Instead of spending millions on recruiting efforts, the LAPD launched a program to fight sagging morale—a compressed work schedule or a "4/10" (a four-day, 10-hour work schedule) for officers. This is the same successful program offered for years by the Los Angeles County Sheriff's Department and other law enforcement agencies in San Diego, Orange County, Long Beach, Burbank, and other places.

When implementing the new 4/10 schedule, supervisors had to be more creative with their scheduling, but it's been worth it. The compressed scheduling programs have greatly increased officer morale and productivity everywhere they've been tried throughout California.

In a survey by PricewaterhouseCoopers, compressed work schedules for law enforcement officers were the number-one suggestion from female officers and third overall among respondents for improving morale. The program is especially popular among younger officers and potential recruits who tend to be very family-focused.

knows of the program. "Sometimes you wonder if you're really making a difference. So when something comes along that actually tells you that you're saving lives by taking certain drastic steps, then you begin to feel good again about why you're out there on the streets in the first place."

Managers Must Re-energize Employee Morale in Tough Environments

As a manager, it's important to acknowledge that sometimes the people you need most in the organization—the ones who will keep you in business and make you look good—are the ones handling the most difficult, most stressful, and often most

> ⚠️ **CAUTION!**
>
> ### It's Time for Managers to Do Better
>
> Employees in every position of every organization deserve to be treated with respect and dignity. Employees will no longer stay in an abusive environment where they must tolerate unreasonable stress or neglect. Managers now know better; therefore, it's expected that they do better on every count. The bar has been raised and successful managers know they must reach it or surpass it, if they are to survive in this competitive world.

unappreciated jobs. They're the workers you can't afford to lose because you've neglected to tell them or show them they're valued and appreciated every single day. These are the workers who are often the hardest to replace and can be the most critical to the overall success of the organization—like those pot washers at the Four Seasons Hotel.

What's Your Approach?

Whatever your approach to handling the toughest of employee morale cases, as manager you must invest whatever time and energy is required to keep those people feeling good about themselves and their jobs. Point out the big picture. Explain to them the direct impact of their efforts on the organization's success. Translate it into dollars whenever possible. For instance: "Susan, you prevented two accidents from happening this month in your department by enforcing safety standards. I estimate you saved the company more than $50,000 by taking fast and decisive action. Thank you. We appreciate your quick thinking more than you know."

This is where you need to spend your energies in order to repair or improve morale in challenging times and in even more challenging environments.

Forget the Prima Donnas

Forget about focusing on the company prima donnas. Too often managers spend inordinate amounts of time dealing with problem employees, instead of proactively managing and working to retain their most valued workers. If you fall into this trap, you could wind up paying the price for your indifference by losing key people at the worst of times.

So start by initiating employee vitality wherever you need it most and whenever you have the chance to do so.

Manager's Checklist for Chapter 7

❏ Instill a sense of meaning and value for each person at every level, not just the top dogs.

❏ Acknowledge that every worker defines his or her level of success differently—and then respect those differences.

❏ Understand that not everyone wants to be in a position of greater responsibility.

❏ Create a feeling of belonging.

❏ Give workers the tools they need to do the job.

❏ Corporate values can drive morale and keep it high in tough times.

❏ Statistics and other important feedback on employee successes can help create more effective internal programs that, when successful, will bolster morale.

❏ Take time to explain to employees the direct impact of their efforts on the organization's success. Translate that value into dollars when possible.

Employees Want and Need a Manager Who Cares

How would you like it if your employees were to wake up every morning, bounce out of bed, and feel happy and excited about going to work before they even had their first cup of coffee? Do you think it's even possible? That's exactly what John Thompson did for 15 years while working in New York City for a midsize Madison Avenue advertising agency.

"People assumed because I worked on Madison Avenue that I was pulling in the big bucks, but that couldn't have been further from the truth. I was a copywriter the first few years I was in New York and, believe me, it's a competitive business there," says Thompson. "Copywriters are a dime a dozen in that city. I really had to stretch every dollar to live in the city and work in the business, but it wasn't the money that made me passionate about what I did for a living or kept me there all those years. It was the love of my job and the love and concern that my manager had for all of us in our department.

"What people don't realize is that employees leave managers, not companies," Thompson observes. "Believe it or not, I only left the agency because my manager died. Otherwise, I know I'd still be there. He's the one who created the high-morale atmosphere and made us all feel special, not the agency itself," emphasizes Thompson. "He gave each employee a soft place to fall in a sometimes hard place to do business."

Thompson says he gets sick and tired of reading about how managers have to be continually convinced that employees are really more interested in how they're being treated than in a bigger paycheck. "When you think about it, most employees want the same basic things from their managers that kids want from their parents—love, clear and consistent expectations, trust, and encouragement and support for their growth and development." He adds, "It seems simple but it's very powerful at the same time because when managers can give these things to their employees, they create an emotional tie that is very strong and really gets people excited and enthusiastic about their work."

> **Gallup Gets It**
>
> **Smart Managing**
>
> The Gallup Organization knows that the greatest source of satisfaction for workers is both emotional and personal. According to this highly reputable organization, the single most important variable in employee productivity and loyalty isn't money or benefits, but rather the quality of the relationship between employees and their supervisors and managers.

What Do Employees Want Most?

It's time managers started quarreling with conventional wisdom when it comes to what they think employees want most from their jobs in order to be fulfilled and happy. This point is well made in the book *First, Break All the Rules: What the World's Greatest Managers Do Differently* by Marcus Buckingham and Curt Coffman (New York: Simon & Schuster, 1999).

After 25 years and interviews with one million workers, the duo developed 12 key questions that address the most desirable and emotional outcomes of employees, giving managers the opportunity to get a handle on their employees' greatest internal and emotional needs. Buckingham and Coffman believe

12 Smart Questions to Ask Your Employees

TOOLS How does your workplace rate? Ask your employees to answer these 12 questions developed by Marcus Buckingham and Curt Coffman for their book, *First, Break All the Rules: What the World's Greatest Managers Do Differently* (New York: Simon & Schuster, 1999).

Answer each question from 1 to 5 (1 = "Strongly Disagree" and 5 = "Strongly Agree").

1. Do I know what is expected of me at work?
2. Do I have the materials and equipment I need to do my work right?
3. At work, do I have the opportunity to do what I do best every day?
4. In the last seven days, have I received recognition or praise for doing good work?
5. Does my supervisor, or someone at work, seem to care about me as a person?
6. Is there someone at work who encourages my development?
7. At work, do my opinions seem to count?
8. Does the mission/purpose of my company make me feel my job is important?
9. Are my co-workers committed to doing quality work?
10. Do I have a best friend at work?
11. In the last six months, has someone at work talked to me about my progress?
12. This last year, have I had opportunities at work to learn and grow?

that a manager can make strong predictions about a worker's performance by allowing him or her to answer 12 basic questions (Sidebar, "12 Smart Questions to Ask Your Employees"). Employees who answered all 12 questions most positively were 50% more likely to work in business units with lower employee turnover, 38% more likely to work in more productive business units, and 56% more likely to work in business units with high customer loyalty.

So, think for a moment about each of your employees. For each one, ask this basic question: What matters most here to him or her? If you don't know, how can you effectively show that you care?

Get Ready, Get Set, Get Assessing

Lois is a team leader at a cellular telephone company in St. Louis, Missouri. For a few months, one of her most productive employees seemed unhappy and off her game. The employee's low morale and lack of enthusiasm for new product promotions and company expansion started to affect others on the team negatively. So Lois decided to take action.

"I just figured in this competitive marketplace that she was probably unhappy with her salary and commission structure," says Lois. "Some of our competitors have snatched up a few of our people by giving them more money and perks. So before she got a chance to give me her resignation, I thought I'd beat her to the punch and increase her salary and commission. Then," says Lois, "two weeks later, she gave notice that she was leaving and I was livid. I kept asking myself, 'What did I miss? What went wrong?'"

Never Assume When You Can Assess

The problem here is actually pretty simple and straightforward. Lois made an assumption about what it would take to boost this employee's morale on the job. She just figured that it had to be money. After all, what else could it be?

The lesson Lois quickly learned was that money is rarely the reason why an employee's morale hits bottom or why employees leave their jobs. What Lois should have done when she became aware of the employee's lack of motivation would have been quick, easy, and free—she should have asked her employee what was wrong and what needed to be done to boost her energy and morale back to normal. Had Lois done this first, she would have discovered early on that an increase in pay or commission wasn't going to make a difference. Money wasn't the issue at all. Instead, she would have learned that this employee was going through a divorce and needed a more flexible schedule in order to spend more time with her children. Her top priority wasn't money; it was balancing home and work. So she found an environment that catered to those needs, leaving a job that offered her more money.

There's another thing that Lois could have done early on to maintain morale and keep this productive employee. She could have assessed her employees' needs and wants on the job. If more supervisors and managers would do this up front, they would save themselves a lot of time, money, and turnover.

When managers ask up front what employees need to be more productive, perform at peak levels, and keep morale high, guess what? Employees will tell them! It's not a secret. Can you imagine how you might have felt if your manager would have asked you these questions early on in your career? Would you have felt more valued as a worker? Would being asked these questions have given you a sense of being cared about? Would you have felt special and more enthusiastic about your job as a result? If your answers are yes, then you've just validated the importance of assessing employees' needs early in the game.

Turn Employees On with This Easy Assessment

Use the assessment tool, "What Matters Most to You?" to determine what motivates each employee and what each employee considers most meaningful. When you know what matters most to an employee, you can keep the momentum going and keep morale high. Then you can prevent problems.

But you won't know if you don't ask! So have your employees complete the assessment.

What Matters Most to You?

Ask employees to assign a number to each item listed in terms of what motivates them and keeps their morale consistently high, using a scale from 1 (lowest) to 4 (highest). Then, after they've each rated all the items, ask them to narrow the list down to their top three. Finally, after they've each picked their top three, have them select and circle the single most important morale booster from their top three picks—and prepare to be surprised at what really motivates your workers.

4 3 2 1   1. My manager showing care and concern for me as a person

4 3 2 1   2. Good working relationship with my manager

4 3 2 1   3. Feeling empowered

```
4 3 2 1   4. Manager's ability to make decisions
4 3 2 1   5. Manager who walks the talk
4 3 2 1   6. Recognition of my efforts
4 3 2 1   7. Delegation of responsibility to me
4 3 2 1   8. Being promoted
4 3 2 1   9. Customer contact
4 3 2 1  10. Compensation
4 3 2 1  11. Getting along with others
4 3 2 1  12. Honest praise
4 3 2 1  13. Helpful and corrective feedback
4 3 2 1  14. Coaching
4 3 2 1  15. The result of a job well done
4 3 2 1  16. Attending social functions with team members
4 3 2 1  17. Being given clear objectives
4 3 2 1  18. Job security
```
Note: This assessment consistently generates similar results. Employees rarely, if ever, rank #10 (compensation) as their highest priority. They most commonly rate highest #1, #2, #6, #12, and #15.

The Time Is Now to Show You Care

Employees want to feel that who they are and what they do matter to their leaders. They want to come to a workplace each day where they feel cared about and loved. Whether you are a team leader, coach, supervisor, manager, director, vice president, or president of an organization, this is your opportunity to touch the lives of those around you every day. As a leader you have the power to promote a more meaningful, joyful and high morale workplace, and the time has never been better.

The Four Ways Managers Show They Care

There are four driving forces that indicate how much a manager really cares about his or her people. Here are the ways managers demonstrate how much they care:

1. They listen.
2. They reward, recognize, and praise.
3. They give and appreciate honest feedback.
4. They instill confidence.

In the rest of this chapter, we'll examine each of those ways of showing that you care about your employees.

Managers Who Listen to Their Employees Keep Morale Up, Up, Up

It's said that all managers should "learn to love to listen." Why? Because managers who love to listen to their employees achieve four critical objectives:

1. They make their employees feel important and valued.
2. They build confidence among their employees because the employees feel heard.
3. They model good communication skills.
4. They make their employees feel worthy and respected.

It's important to note here that a manager who's mastered the art of listening also knows how to ask pertinent questions, the kind of questions that tell employees that the manager cares about what they're saying and wants to gather more information. So be sure to ask who, what, where, when, why, and how questions. Then show you care by seeking additional information by asking questions like these:

- Can you tell me a little more about that?
- Who else will participate in this?

TRICKS OF THE TRADE
How Managers Who Are Good Listeners Act

- Good listeners assume the "listening position" by sitting up straight and sometimes leaning forward as if to say with their body language, "I'm very interested in what you are saying."
- Good listeners actually enjoy listening and participate in the process by smiling, nodding, laughing, or showing other expressions of affirmation, empathy, and appreciation.
- Good listeners focus all their attention on the other person. They are considerate and courteous when listening to someone else. They don't let distractions get in the way.
- Good listeners offer their input and suggestions after the other person has spoken. They are not just waiting for their turn to talk next.

- Where will this take place?
- When can we expect to see changes occur?
- How can I help?

When you want to summarize and restate what an employee has just communicated, try the following questions:

- Do I understand you to mean that ...?
- Let's summarize the important points.
- How would you restate that message for our group?
- Am I clear in understanding that you would like ...?

Bridging the Gap

In a survey conducted by O'Connor Kenny Partners in 1999, HR directors listed the top 10 skills that managers need for organizational success. At the top of their list, tied with interpersonal skills, was listening—outranking such essentials as conflict management, persuasion and motivation, writing, presentation skills, and reading.

And yet, in a survey by the Hay Group that polled over 1,000,000 employees in over 2,000 companies, only about one in three people responded favorably when asked how well their managers or companies listened to them. Obviously there's a wide gap between what managers should be doing and what their employees perceive as happening.

But you have the power to reach out to the people who work for you, to listen to them and learn from them. Remember: it's not so much the words you say during the exchange as it is the fact that you as a manager are listening to your employees. When you listen, you're affirming that person and showing that you care. When you listen, you're working to bridge the gap.

Rewards, Recognition, and Praise Are Links to Higher Morale and Performance

Philosopher William James said, "The deepest craving in human nature is the craving to be appreciated." And he was right. When employees feel appreciated they perform and produce at their best. When they don't feel appreciated, there's often a drop in both performance and production across the board.

Employee rewards and incentive programs have become a multimillion dollar industry filled with award plaques, recognition banquets, prizes from movie tickets to BMWs, exotic travel, gift certificates, and free dinners at Morton's Steakhouse. But even as much as employees love these prizes, one form of recognition remains the most cost-effective and easy way to sing some-body's praises—the good old-fashioned pat on the back!

Make It Real Praise—Not Phony Flattery

The best recognition is real praise, from the heart. It's not about the phony flattery that some managers use to manipulate employees into doing better work or more work or both. Employees know when managers are manipulating them with phony flattery in order to get something in return—"Oh, my

---

TRICKS OF THE TRADE

Affordable Ways to Reward, Recognize, and Praise Employees

In his best-selling book, *1001 Ways to Reward Employees* (New York: Workman Publishing, 1994), Bob Nelson offers up a multitude of fun, stimulating, low-cost, and proven strategies for bumping up employee morale. Here are a few:

- **Time off.** Employees love time off work. It's a precious and valu-able commodity in our busy world.
- **Recognition items.** These include trophies, engraved plaques, watches, and other customized gifts.
- **Parties and other celebrations.** Examples include everything from Margarita Happy Hour to Halloween parties and birthday cel-ebrations, from laugh-a-day staff challenges and fun committees to grill-your-boss cookouts and Felix and Oscar awards for the neatest and messiest workers.
- **Praise.** No-cost, on-the-spot praise remains the most popular of all informal recognition efforts. You can just say, "Thank you for a job well done," you can write out little notes of praise, and you can recognize an employee in front of coworkers. It's all good.

manager just told me what a good job I did on the Bronson Report, so I guess she'll be wanting me to work an extra shift again this week" or "This afternoon the boss thanked me for working so hard on the marketing campaign, then immediately asked me to stay late so we could finish it."

When managers use praise to manipulate, they lose respect and credibility when it comes to giving real compliments, because the employees are always suspecting underlying motives. When you praise an employee, pay attention to the reaction, to the person's expression and words. It's a good way to detect how your employees perceive praise coming from you. If they seem to be "waiting for the other shoe to drop," as one employee put it, then you may be guilty of praising with underlying motives.

Do It Now!

Praise is best when it comes immediately. When you notice that an employee has done an outstanding job or you find out about an exceptional effort, that's the time for praise. Never withhold your praise just because you're waiting for bigger and better accomplishments. Saving recognition and praise for the big wins isn't what boosts employee morale; it's getting noticed for the constant small wins along the way that keeps people up and wanting to do their best.

> ⚠️ **CAUTION!**
> ### Don't Hold Back When an Employee Deserves Praise
> You should never hesitate to praise an employee simply because your boss may never praise you. And don't use the excuse, "I expect my people to do a good job without having to be praised for it all the time." That attitude might have worked 30 years ago, but not in today's competitive marketplace. Employees will always do a better job if they receive consistent and ongoing recognition for a job well done. Kenneth Blanchard, coauthor of *The One Minute Manager* (New York: Berkley Books, 1983), asserts, "The key to developing people is to catch them doing something right." Then praise them—immediately.

Giving Feedback to Employees Builds Morale

You can't always praise your employees, of course. Sometimes you need to provide feedback that's not all positive. But if you do it right, that feedback can be good for morale.

Just about everything we learn to do well we learn by receiving feedback from someone. Whether it's riding a bike or learning to swim, developing coaching skills or creating an effective strategic plan, we benefit from helpful feedback in some way. And when a manager makes it a point to give employees regular feedback, he or she is actually sending a much bigger message. The message says, "I care about you and I want to help you to develop your talents."

Managers who care about helping their employees develop should know how to effectively provide these four types of feedback:

Smart Managing

Big Benefits of Feedback

What are some of the benefits of feedback? Consider these:

- Feedback creates trust.
- Feedback encourages cooperation and collaboration.
- Feedback clarifies for employees what it means to do a job well and what is unacceptable.
- Feedback inspires employees to develop new skills.
- Feedback builds self-confidence.

Type 1: Frequent and Sincere
Type 2: Fast and Action-Oriented
Type 3: Helpful and Corrective
Type 4: Empathetic and Sensitive

Type 1: Frequent and Sincere. The best managers have lots of sincere and positive feedback to offer when they see good things happening. They know that employees thrive on frequent and positive input and that sincerity is the key to delivering their message.

Here's an example: "Super job, Kevin! This project wasn't easy from the start. You had a lot of obstacles to overcome and you did it. Keep up the good work." In this example, the manager is not just giving positive input but also making it clear that he or she has paid attention to the difficulty of the project and respects what the employee has accomplished.

Type 2: Fast and Action-Oriented. This type of feedback is often called "speedback" because time is of the essence. Top managers know how to use this technique to create a high morale work environment because they know that employees get pumped up when their managers are spontaneous and waste no time giving them fast feedback on the spot! Here are some examples of this type of feedback:

- "That looks frustrating, Mark. I have some templates in my office I think may help. Let's go get them now and see if it makes the job easier. Then, I'll get back to you this afternoon to see how you're doing."
- "Hold everything, Jane! I love your enthusiasm, but I think you may want to try a softer approach first. Let's sit down and I'll share with you a personal experience I had last year and you can tell me your thoughts as well."
- "Hi, Lucas. I'm calling right after reading your e-mail to let you know that I still don't have all the details or answers to your questions. I thought you'd appreciate knowing this right away. I do think I'll have something for you by 4:00 today."
- "I just got your memo, Todd, and I wanted to respond immediately to say that I think it would be best for us to follow up on this right away. When can you go over this with me?"

Type 3: Helpful and Corrective. The point here is to be constructive and not destructive. Helpful and corrective feedback should be easy to swallow. It's a method that tells someone you care and that you are willing to take the time to point out areas of needed improvement and show that person how to use his or her greatest strengths to accomplish the task successfully. Helpful and corrective feedback should never be delivered with anger or aggression. Think before you speak and plan the appropriate corrective feedback. For example: "Tony, learning this equipment can take some time. Let me show you some of the shortcuts I learned when I started here." Or, "You seem to be struggling with this computer program, Louise. I think it would be good to partner with Ben for a few days. He's got a real knack with this stuff and has coached several of our people, like Mike for instance." Corrective and helpful feedback gives employees the opportunity to learn and feel comfortable not knowing all the moves or having all the answers.

Type 4: Empathetic and Sensitive. Giving feedback can be awkward when someone is extra sensitive to the input or has other challenges. It's your job as the manager to gauge when it's appropriate to give empathetic and sensitive feedback to someone. Here are some hints:

- Don't negate your feedback by adding something like "Well, it's about time."
- Don't leave anyone in the group out when you're giving feedback to everyone else. You might be thinking, "Oh this doesn't apply to her," but that's not the point. If you're addressing the group, don't exclude anyone. This can really affect an employee's feelings negatively.
- Never—even jokingly—embarrass or put someone down in order to make a point about your feedback.
- Most of all, be empathetic with employees when giving them feedback. What do you think it must feel like to them? Put yourself in their shoes first and remember the advice of Stephen R. Covey, from his best-selling book *The 7 Habits of Highly Effective People* (New York: Fireside, 1989): "Seek first to understand, then to be understood."

When asked, most people will say that they sincerely welcome feedback because it helps them to improve. The issue, however, is not the feedback itself, but the environment in which the feedback comes and how it's delivered. As manager, it's your responsibility to help establish a safe and respectful workplace for giving and receiving feedback of all kinds. High morale workplaces are noted for this.

Keys to Providing Feedback Most Effectively
Before delivering feedback of any kind, first ask your
employees these questions:
  1. How would you like to receive feedback from me?
  2. What specifically would you most like to receive feedback on?
  3. How can I help you feel more comfortable about receiving correc-
     tive and constructive feedback?
  4. How can I best give you feedback as we go along?
  5. Since you seem quite busy, how do you recommend I get this
     information to you in a timely manner?

Getting Feedback from Employees Builds Morale

When a manager chooses to willingly accept feedback from his
or her employees, he or she not only becomes a better manager, but also starts building a new level of communications skills
and shows employees that their input is worth something.

Do Something with the Feedback You Get

It's always smart to acknowledge and consider the feedback you
get from employees, whether you choose to act on it or not. By
acknowledging to your employees that you appreciate the time
and effort they put into offering their ideas and suggestions,
you're subtly building stronger morale and confidence
among your workers.

Consider this. Every
time an employee offers
you feedback, you have
another opportunity to
improve the environment
and improve yourself. In
fact, managers can accel-
erate their own growth and
development by seeking
out feedback from the
team and other reliable
sources and then using

Facts on Feedback

Smart Managing

Fact #1: Feedback from
employees gives a manager
his or her greatest opportunity for
overcoming challenges.
Fact #2: Feedback provides managers
with valuable information that can
help improve morale.
Fact #3: Feedback can uncover underlying problems so the manager can
solve them before they worsen.
Fact #4: Feedback helps make managers better listeners.

those ideas to suggest changes for improving performance and the workplace.

Feedback—the Gift

Think of feedback (all kinds) as a gift and encourage your employees to do the same. Tell employees that feedback offers enormous life-changing value. One small piece of feedback can alter the course of a person's life or the course of the work environment toward higher morale and initiative. When we choose to learn from the feedback we receive—positive or constructive—we can use the gift we've been given to improve performance, productivity, and morale.

Get "Up and Go" Model for Feedback

Get...
   Understand others.
* Recognize how each employee prefers to receive your feedback.
* Create a safe environment for fostering feedback.
* Adjust your approach for the person to whom you are addressing the feedback.

Plan the appropriate message for your feedback.
* It's not just *what* you say, but also *how:* monitor your tone and volume.
* Think before you speak.
* Separate facts from feelings.

and

Give helpful and constructive feedback in a timely manner.
* Adjust your style when necessary. Be empathetic and sensitive.
* Be aware of your nonverbal communication and body language.
* Be constructive, not destructive.

Obtain feedback willingly and with appreciation.
* Show that you're genuinely thankful and appreciative.
* Ask questions that demonstrate your interest and concern.
* Be open-minded. There's no right or wrong feedback—just feedback.

Note: Give this model to your employees. You may want to reproduce and laminate it as a wallet-size card and encourage employees to reference it often. Do the same yourself.

Confidence Is Key in Achieving High Morale

Here's a twist on an old adage. You can give someone a fish and he won't be hungry. Or you can teach someone to fish and he'll never be hungry again. But if you create an environment in which all people are encouraged to take initiative and become self-directed learners, assured of themselves and their abilities, then they will find ways to teach themselves to fish and gain loads of self-confidence in the process that will build the morale of all the people in the fishing village.

Morale in the workplace depends on the self-esteem and self-confidence of the people who work there. But the organization and/or any manager cannot bestow upon an employee self-esteem and self-confidence. It's not an abracadabra kind of thing. Sure, there are some managers who think that a job or a promotion will increase confidence. But any effects of such actions on self-confidence don't last for long. As generous as these actions may appear, they do not guarantee that an employee will be self-confident. That's got to come from within the employee first, not from the manager. A person must believe in himself or herself before even taking the job or accepting the promotion.

What the manager can provide, however, is a healthy atmosphere and opportunities for self-confidence to flourish, an environment where strong self-esteem and a positive self-concept are appreciated and motivate top performance. Great managers have a knack for seeing the potential in someone and then helping that person believe in his or her potential and develop it. As the manager, you can help co-create with your employees a workplace that nurtures confidence and gives them the opportunity to put that confidence to work. When that happens, you've not only instilled a feeling of greater ability and potential in others, but you've also promoted higher employee morale in the workplace.

Smart managers create environments that promote confidence. This shows their employees that they care about them.

Smart Managing

Getting Published Is a Great Confidence Booster

To help build employee confidence and boost morale, find venues like newspapers and trade journals to publish their stories. Here are some tips:

- When an employee receives an award or achieves something significant, send out a press release to the local media—and then send it to the employee's hometown newspaper along with his or her picture.
- Submit an employee's unusual or special story to the local press or an industry trade journal. For example, when an employee donated a kidney to a fellow employee, the company contacted a local publication. The published story made everybody in the company proud of the generous employee and pleased that the community knew about the deed.
- Have your company take out a full-page ad in the local newspaper to thank a list of employees for a major accomplishment and for making the organization look good.
- Use company publications and newsletters. At H.J. Heinz, internal publications and annual reports are used regularly to brag about employees and even publish their poetry.

What do you think employee confidence levels were like in the department where John Thompson worked at the Madison Avenue ad agency? You can bet they were pretty high and that they remained high through the years.

The Winning Formula

When you put into play the four critical driving forces that demonstrate how much you really care about your people, the many benefits come naturally. Listen carefully to your employees. Reward, recognize, and praise them for a job well done. Give them honest feedback and invite, appreciate, and use feedback from them. Help build confidence and create an environment that nurtures a healthy self-esteem in every employee. Then you've got a winning formula for high morale.

Manager's Checklist for Chapter 8

❏ Employees don't leave *companies*; they leave *managers*.

❏ Never assume what an employee needs or wants without assessing the situation first.

❏ Employees want to feel that who they are and what they do matter to their leaders.

❏ When managers show they care, they listen; they reward, recognize, and praise; they give and appreciate honest feedback; and they instill confidence.

❏ Never hold back on praise. Look for ways to catch employees doing something right as often as possible— and then praise them.

❏ Feedback should be frequent and sincere, fast and action-oriented, helpful and creative, and empathetic and sensitive.

❏ Smart managers create environments that nurture support and instill confidence in their workers.

Winning Back Morale in Emotional Times— What to Do When Tragedy Strikes

The Chinese have two distinct characters for the word "crisis." One means danger and the other opportunity.

Tough times call for real leadership and therein lie both the danger and the opportunity—managers who are willing to face adversity, rather than shrink from it, and then somehow in the process create greater hope and higher morale because of it. As a manager or supervisor, this may well be the greatest challenge and responsibility of your career.

According to Lexicon Communications, a strategic PR and crisis management consulting firm headquartered in Los Angeles, every company—large or small, public or private—

runs the risk of confronting a crisis. The firm estimates that the most forward-thinking managers are the ones who will be best equipped to handle the impact of an unexpected crisis on their employees, drastically affecting long-term employee morale.

Simply being aware of the resources available can be critical. Lexicon takes the position that, like the two Chinese characters suggest, a crisis is a turning point from which prepared managers are capable of creating opportunity in times of danger.

Employees' Expectations of Managers Are Higher than Ever

Surveys show that workers around the globe are experiencing unprecedented levels of anxiety in the workplace and, as a result, employees have much higher expectations of their managers when it comes to helping them cope with catastrophe or ease their anxiety.

Every workday, somewhere in an organization, there are employees who are being forced to confront their fears when they go to the office. You might be thinking that the workplace has become a target for terror. It hasn't. The real targets are employee morale, joy, and optimism.

Xerox—No Stranger to Crisis

Employees and managers of the copier giant, Xerox, have had to deal with their own crises. In 1999 seven Xerox workers were shot and killed by a former employee at the company's Honolulu location. One manager says that the tragic situation helped prepare the company to take specific steps to calm its employees' fears since September 11. The Stamford-based organization worked constantly to keep communications flowing and to stay connected to everyone. For example, Xerox posted information regarding 9/11 on a daily basis on the company intranet. It also posted helpful information related to employees' travel fears, such as advisories or state department warnings on specific destinations. And when employees became concerned about safety issues, they were told how to contact company security for additional assistance.

Managers Ask, "How Can I Win Back Employee Morale?"

In the aftermath of 9/11, managers in companies of all sizes will continue to ask for some time to come, "How can I win back employee morale?" It's important to point out that regaining employee morale after tragedy strikes was a management concern well before the unimaginable terrorist attacks on the United States. However, it somehow took the enormity of these attacks to shed greater light on how trauma can so destructively affect workplace morale in order to remind us that we must take care of our people, first and foremost, especially when they have suffered heartache, fear, and uncertainty about the future.

> **TOOLS**
>
> **Words of Encouragement**
>
> "You gain strength, courage and confidence by every experience by which you really stop to look fear in the face. You are able to say to yourself, 'I lived through this horror, I can take the next thing that comes along.'"
> —Eleanor Roosevelt

Managers Look to Seminars as a Helpful Resource

A customer service manager at one of the world's largest financial services firms, located just one block away from New York's World Trade Center, told me in late 2001:

> The first few months, it seemed like everyone was in shock. Now the reality of what has happened has sunk in and employees are having an extremely difficult time dealing with it all and concentrating on their work. Some can barely function. And as managers, we've never dealt with anything of this magnitude ourselves. We're still suffering too. It seems one of our biggest challenges is building back morale in the face of everything that's happened.

It wasn't long after this interview took place that this manager contacted me about customizing an employee seminar for their workers and a separate seminar for their management team. The programs were well received and employees quickly let management know that they felt like their calls for help were being heard and that many of their needs were being met. In addition, the company's managers were able to deal with their own feelings as leaders and at the same time gain additional tools and techniques for helping their employees continue to heal and move forward.

I want to stress here that this chapter is not about terrorism or the events of September 11. However, it would have been impossible to write this chapter without discussing the unspeakable events that took place in our country on that dreadful day in September 2001 and interviewing some of the managers who continue struggling to rebuild workplace morale. In

Dealing with Disaster

The following are seminar outlines for employees and for managers and supervisors. Each program included a take-away workbook for participants. As a manager, you may want to consider providing similar programs to meet your workers' needs.

Employees' Seminar: Content Outline
Title: Hope, Faith, and a Plan for a Better Tomorrow
Welcome/Introduction
- Look How Far We've Come—Moving Toward Your Authentic Self
- Hold Hope High—Winning Back Employee Morale
- What Life Could Be: Eight Ways to Stronger Self-Esteem
- The Human Spirit—That's the Voyage
- Celebrate You! Passion, Purpose, and Providence
Closing Comments

Managers' Seminar: Content Outline
Title: Building Back Morale in Emotional Times—When Tragedy Strikes
Welcome/Introduction
- Miracles of a High Morale Workplace
- How World-Class Managers Build Morale in Tough Times
- Recalibrating What's Important
- Coaching People Toward a New Path
- Managers: Dispensers of Hope and Vision
Closing Comments

Prepare for the Worst, Hope for the Best
According to Steven Fink, president of the crisis management firm Lexicon Communications and author of *Crisis Management: Planning for the Inevitable* (New York: AMACOM, 1986, hardcover; Campbell, CA: iUniverse, 2000, paperback), it is the element of surprise that is most unsettling to leaders when confronted by sudden catastrophe. "The savviest chief executive in the world often falls victim to a kind of paralysis when a crisis strikes." His suggestion: every major executive and manager should prepare by reading at least one book on crisis management.

addition, this chapter will focus on a handful of real workplace crises and describe how courageous managers have chosen to effectively lead their employees through the toughest of times.

The fact is that workplace disasters are ever increasing. It's my hope, therefore, that if one day you find yourself faced with leading your workers out of disaster, where emotions run high and morale is severely impaired, you will be better equipped to handle such a situation because of the information and examples provided in this chapter.

The Day That Changed the World

It became a new Day of Infamy, more terrifying than the attack on Pearl Harbor in 1941 or the savage Okalahoma City federal building bombing of 1995 or the World Trade Center basement bombing in 1993. Our nation's symbol of military might, the Pentagon, was attacked and the once gleaming twin towers of the World Trade Center, a signature skyline of American financial strength recognized the world over, are gone forever. But this nation's human spirit showed the strength of a people united in patriotic pride and unshakeable resolve.

The tragedy of 9/11 awoke a sleeping giant within each of us. A giant that many of us might have forgotten lay asleep until the horror we experienced caused it to rise up in the form of extraordinary valor and heroism demonstrated daily by firefighters, police officers, service workers, medical personnel, construction workers, clergy, and ordinary citizens. The nation rallied with unprecedented spirit, morale, and sacrifice, while Americans stood strong and tall in their resolve.

People Are the Backbone

The backbone of the nation, like the backbone

of your organization, is and has always been its people. From the ashes of fallen buildings, the spirit of America has risen and it is up to managers and other leaders to harness that undeniable spirit and commitment in any way they can to build hope for a better tomorrow and faith in what lies ahead for us all.

When It Takes More than Faith to Win Back Employee Morale

People react in many different ways when tragedy strikes. Some quit their jobs and look for safer havens, even if it's for less money. Others may be confused, angry, and doubtful about their work, their employers, and their futures. Some will sit back until they see something they can believe in again or until faith returns to others around them.

As a manager, you've got to remember that when tragedy strikes, it hits something much bigger than our sense of well-being and security—it's an assault on our belief systems, ideas, goals, and visions for a prosperous future. These are just a few of the effects that workers must deal with.

Employees Look to Their Leaders When Tragedy Strikes

Tragedies of every kind become direct attacks on our faith as people and proportionately impact employee morale. On top of this, cynics may wonder if there is anything left to be enthusiastic about or to believe in.

(After the Columbine incident in Littleton, Colorado, parents around the country began opting for home schooling. There's certainly nothing wrong with home schooling, but the decisions that were made to do so were probably based more on fear than on hope for a better education.)

The point is, when fear takes over, you've lost the battle. Managers lose when their employees give up. Companies lose when employees huddle together in fear and talk about building bomb shelters in their basements, buying gas masks, or stock-piling antibiotics for fear of anthrax or other kinds of chemical contamination.

When tragedy strikes the workplace, employees look to their leaders to give them something to believe in again and to remind them why it's important to keep moving forward. Therefore, managers must be prepared to lead with confidence in times of great uncertainty—even when they themselves feel uncertain. Your every move and demeanor will be observed by your employees when there's a crisis. How will you demonstrate your confidence?

Rudy Giuliani—Unshakeable Confidence in Action

"Show me a hero and I'll write you a tragedy," said F. Scott Fitzgerald. For former New York City mayor, Rudolph Giuliani, the tragedy was written on September 11, 2001. And from that event a hero was born—a man who led the way to winning back the fighting spirit of a city that he often calls "the capital of the world."

After almost being buried alive just a few blocks from the attacks on the World Trade Center, the mayor of New York proved to the world that he could contain and manage the despair of millions with an onslaught of continuous information and inspiration—never substituting one for the other. In the short time that followed, Giuliani, like any manager, was faced with making fast decisions: immediately shutting down parts of the city, creating makeshift command centers and morgues, somehow getting hold of millions of gloves and dust masks, and at the same time protecting the city from more attacks, riots, and other vulnerabilities. The people of New York looked to their leader when catastrophe struck, just as your organization's people will look to you if they get caught up in turmoil and crisis.

> **Managers Lose When Employees Give Up**
> As manager, it's up to you to inspire your workers—even
> in the face of tragedy—to never give up or give in. The
> moment your employees give up, you will lose the battle for regaining
> hope and happiness in your organization. Remind your employees of
> this inspiring exhortation by Winston Churchill, from October 1941,
> when war made the future of Britain uncertain: "Never give in, never
> give in, never, never, never, never—in nothing, great or small, large or
> petty—never give in except to convictions of honour and good sense."

Fighting Back with Confidence in Emotional Times

So how does a manager fight back? What's it going to take to
get employees fired up and motivated after they've experienced
a horrendous event?

One manager of a real estate company where two employees were shot and killed by a disgruntled ex-employee offers
these suggestions on winning back morale in emotional times.

> Of course we were all devastated. We are a tight-knit
> group of workers. It's more like a family here and turnover
> is very low. When this happened there was severe trauma
> to my employees. We all got crisis counseling but after
> that we still needed to get back on the horse, so to speak,
> and it was very hard. Morale was so low and people were
> scared all the time. We purposely used this cowardly
> attack to redirect our intense feelings and anger and to
> regain our high employee morale.
>
> We all agreed that we could win if we used this cow-
> ardly attack as a spur to boost our productivity and not let
> it put us out of business. We owed this to our families, our
> co-workers who lost their lives, and to ourselves.
>
> We wanted to fight back with our attitudes, not our
> anger, for the sake of our employees who lost their lives
> and for the sake of our own mental health.
>
> We created a trust account for the families of our co-
> workers who lost their lives and that motivated us to boost
> sales so that we could all contribute a portion of our com-

missions to the fund and help the families who were left behind.

We set up a college scholarship fund for each of the victim's children.

We continually reminded each other that we all win against terror and crime when each of us creates new opportunities for the firm and our fellow employees, or when one of us gets on a plane and flies to a conference to learn something new and valuable to share with our co-workers, or just by getting up in the morning and coming to work with a positive attitude in honor of those who are no longer with us.

All of these things helped our company to recapture its once extremely high employee morale. It didn't happen quickly, but over time it worked and we got better. We were able to heal ourselves and move on.

Reclaiming Their Freedom from Fear and Anxiety

Managers should remember that when their employees' faith and belief in a brighter future evaporate because of a tragedy, their passion and love for the job can disappear too. Therefore, it's important for managers to focus on what will make life better for everyone. What will it take to make your employees happy and fulfilled once again? When we help our employees reclaim their enthusiasm and think, dream, and reach for the stars again, everything they do becomes more productive, lucrative, and meaningful. The questions to ask are "What is the most worthwhile way we can spend our time?" and "What do we need to do to become whole again?" Then, start doing it.

The Importance of Crisis Debriefing

When tragedy strikes, managers can be extremely influential in helping employees to reclaim their freedom from fear and anxiety just by knowing what resources are available to them. Crisis debriefing, a form of crisis management, has proven to be one very helpful alternative and resource that managers worldwide

Six Tips for Guiding Employees Back to Work

1. Discuss openly security concerns that your employees may be harboring and address them head on.
2. Ask your employees what kinds of information would make them feel more at ease—and then deliver it.
3. Stress the "new normal" way of doing things, acknowledging your understanding that things will never be the same again.
4. Create a "Remembrance Committee" for selecting various ways to structure benevolent involvement, like remembering anniversaries and reaching out to families.
5. Recognize employees who have gone the extra mile and have extended extra effort during times of crisis. Publicly acknowledge out-of-the-ordinary efforts.
6. Keep a healthy balance of work and remembering. It's a fragile time. You don't want to dwell on the negative, but you should encourage employees to remember what happened and balance that time with building back a strong and healthy, high morale workplace.

have learned to depend on again and again.

In incidents ranging from bank robberies and hurricanes to airplane crashes and workplace killings, crisis debriefing is seen as a way to show an organization's compassion. Crisis debriefing can bring order out of chaos by blending therapeutic counseling with consulting. Although this process can be therapeutic, it's important to point out that it's not therapy. Crisis debriefing focuses more on the here and now and how to move forward and live and work productively and happily once again.

Crisis debriefing A "psychological first-aid kit" of emergency counseling designed to help people understand and cope with their reactions to traumatic events.

Be Ready to Mobilize All Resources

It's hard to imagine something terrible happening to those we work with and care about. But suppose you had the power to foresee the services and support that would be available to you and your workers? Wouldn't you feel better prepared to handle a

Where Crisis Management Has Helped in the Past

Times when crisis management techniques have proven enormously helpful in rebuilding workplace morale following a disaster:

- NASA's Space Shuttle Challenger explosion
- Three Mile Island nuclear incident
- Johnson & Johnson's two product tampering tragedies involving Tylenol
- Financial crises of Ohio's S&Ls
- Columbine High School shooting
- World Trade Center and Pentagon terrorist attacks

disaster, should one occur, and to provide swift and effective support and reassurance to your employees?

Well, you have that power. Start preparing now, before something happens. This can make all the difference between a manager who's considered to be a prepared and effective leader and one who's caught up in the chaos and unable to get ahead of the problem or help his or her people cope with catastrophe when they need it most.

Investigate Your Employee Assistance Program

When disaster strikes, managers must quickly mobilize their resources. It's not the time to try to gather information when you're smack in the middle of a major crisis. It's all about action. That means you need to make time now to investigate what resources would be available to you, if necessary.

Start by talking to someone in your organization's employee assistance program (EAP). They should be able to alert you to the firms that your organization contracts with for crisis counseling and other services in the event of an emergency. Visit those companies' Web sites. Find out more about what these resources can offer your workers in various unexpected scenarios. Then share this vital information with your people. Why? Most employees say they need this "just-in-case" information and satisfaction in order to maintain peace of mind.

> **Three-Step Recovery Program**
> An effective tool used by Crisis Management
> International—a virtual organization of more than 1,400
> therapists and psychologists trained in critical incident stress debrief-
> ing—is a Three-Step Recovery Program.
>   In groups of 15 to 20 people, for one or two hours, employees are
> helped through three important steps:
> 1. **Telling stories and sharing feelings.** It's often important for sur-
>   vivors just to tell their stories. This can fulfill employees' needs to
>   be validated in their feelings about what took place. It also becomes
>   a safe place for people to vent.
> 2. **Creating "normalization."** This is when a crisis counselor lis-
>   tens to and reassures employees that their specific range of reac-
>   tions and emotions is considered "normal." This is important reas-
>   surance for participants.
> 3. **Providing information and education.** People who have experi-
>   enced trauma need to know what to expect. How long will it take
>   to heal? How soon should a person return to his or her routine?
>   What signs might indicate the need for more counseling or possibly
>   therapy?

The Human Side of Crisis

One manager of an insurance company's in-house employee
assistance program says, "When tragedy strikes, managers need
to remember that there is a 'human side' to every crisis that must
be dealt with right away. The goal should be to help employees
return as quickly as possible to normal work and normal productivity, or at least what's considered to be the 'new normal.'"
    Sometimes immediate crisis debriefing can help prevent
additional problems for employees, like post-traumatic stress
disorder. The objective is to keep employees from having to use
medications to cope or rely on psychiatric counseling for long
periods of time.

When Life Intervenes

Unfortunately, there's not a book or a plan that can provide you
with all the answers for handling the most unexpected things

> **Key Term**
>
> **Post-traumatic stress disorder** A condition that develops as a result of experiencing a distressing event beyond the normal range of experiences. It affects hundreds of thousands of people who have survived tragedies, such as natural disasters like earthquakes and fires or deliberate disasters such as terrorism, rape, or school and workplace shootings. Post-traumatic stress disorder rarely appears during the trauma itself. The disorder can surface soon after an event or months or even years later. The symptoms of post-traumatic stress disorder include the following:
> - flashbacks, in which the victim relives the traumatic event
> - nightmares
> - insomnia
> - sudden and painful onslaught of emotions associated with the tragedy
> - irritability or emotional outbursts
> - guilt for having survived the crisis when others did not
> - depression
> - general emotional numbness, sometimes causing the victim to withdraw from others
> - frequent use of drugs and alcohol

that life can throw at you. When life intervenes, it intervenes. And no matter how high employee morale runs in your organization or how energized employees appear, everyone—including you—is subject to the unexpected, including tragedies. When life intervenes, managers must deal with it and take action. In the words of Joan Baez, "Action is the antidote to despair."

Two Kinds of Managers in a Crisis—Which One Are You?

So which managers succeed at winning back shattered employee morale and which do not? There seem to be two kinds. Some managers can't seem to rebound from major setbacks or overcome obstacles and some managers rise above it all, refusing defeat and reclaiming their people's victory.

What's the difference?

The managers who help their employees overcome

tragedies are well prepared. They know how to quickly mobilize help in a hurry. Then they make a deliberate and conscious effort to draw on the passion, energy, and inspiration of the people around them. They keeping workers well informed and they always tell the truth about the situation, not candy-coating critical information no matter how painful.

Will you be that kind of manager in a crisis?

Navigating Toward Survival and Hope

Managers who instinctively and repeatedly instill feelings of hope and positive morale into their employees will find these feelings sustaining them and their people through the best and worst of times. These instincts become a manager's inner compass for navigating toward survival, confronting problems with greater confidence, and making resilience a personal declaration, eventually becoming an ongoing source of revitalization and even heroism when necessary.

Real-World Navigator of Survival and Hope

Dr. Pam Hinds, director of nursing research at St. Jude Children's Research Hospital in Memphis, Tennessee, has been navigating the survival and hope of her patients, their families, and her staff for more than 17 years. In an environment where catastrophic childhood illnesses are a daily reality, Dr. Hinds has helped to create an environment for her staff where hope and high morale are the orders of the day.

"I point out to people that this work is not about focusing on the intensity of sadness and death that can result from these illnesses. Instead we learn to focus on the moment-to-moment miracles that happen here, at St. Jude's, every single day. If you stop focusing on all of the remarkable possibilities, there can be chaos," says Dr. Hinds.

Here are some of the suggestions that Dr. Hinds offers her staff when it comes to sustaining high morale in an environment where fear for what might be and hope for what can be come together on a daily basis.

- Never sacrifice human connection for productivity.
- Honor every relationship.
- Be a real person to those who need you, get involved with their lives.
- Focus on what is most meaningful to others and meet those human needs as best you can.
- Understand that much can be said with few words.
- Have a mission, because when the mission is clear, like it is at St. Jude's—"to find cures for children with catastrophic illnesses through research and treatment"—you will draw the right people to the organization.
- In the midst of extreme intensity and sadness, always point to the many miracles of survival that surround you.
- Remember that everything good that you do on the job goes beyond the walls of where you work.
- Understand that even dying patients have hope and it is your job to help sustain that hope.
- Look to the future and share your hope and belief in miracles.

Manager's Checklist for Chapter 9

❑ The Chinese have two distinct characters for the word "crisis." One means danger and the other opportunity.

❑ The odds are good that one day you will be confronted with a workplace crisis. Being prepared ahead of time will be the key to responding successfully.

❑ The workplace isn't the target for terror. The real targets are employee morale, joy, and optimism.

❑ People are the backbone of every organization.

❑ Employees look to their leaders for guidance when tragedy strikes.

❑ Winning back employee morale takes the confidence to lead during emotional times.

❑ Crisis debriefing can be a powerful and effective resource when coping with catastrophe and it demonstrates an organization's compassion for their people.

❏ Managers must be ready to mobilize resources at a moment's notice.

❏ Employees want "just-in-case" information in order to maintain peace of mind.

❏ Managers should take the approach that there is a human side to every crisis.

10

Engendering Hope, Trust, Faith, and Belief in a Better Tomorrow

U p until a few years ago, most managers trivialized the importance of certain workplace topics, like hope, trust, and faith, when it came to managing people, particularly in larger organizations. That's all changing. Today, even top business schools, like Harvard Business School and Northwestern University's Kellogg Graduate School, offer entire management courses featuring curriculum and case studies focused on these exact subjects.

By now you've caught on to the continuous message woven through the chapters of this book: it's not enough to encourage employees toward higher productivity and performance. Great managers evaluate the whole person's needs and, in the process, are able to better grasp the importance of engendering hope, trust, faith, and the belief in a better tomorrow. It is for these reasons that employees are drawn to a specific organization's goals and will more readily buy into a manager's long-term vision.

> ## Oprah Teaches Grad Students a New Brand of Management
>
> The stereotype of theory-based business school curriculum was broken at Northwestern University's Kellogg Graduate School when Oprah Winfrey introduced a 10-week course called "Dynamics of Leadership." The program—designed by adjunct professors Winfrey and Stedman Graham—focused on topics such as knowing your whole self, identifying your beliefs as a leader, maintaining faith in yourself, finding hope, instilling trust, and personal visioning. The top business school attests that this was one of the most popular programs ever offered and that students flocked to class to learn these important management lessons, making way for a new kind of management program at the institution.

Managers Hold Hope High

Great leaders honor the value of hope. One notable example was Winston Churchill. Following World War II, a reporter asked the Prime Minister of England what the greatest weapon had been against Germany. Churchill responded, "It was what England's greatest weapon has always been. Hope."

As a manager, you can use hope as your greatest weapon. How are you currently using hope in your organization to build employee morale? How do you think employees having greater hope could make the overall work environment more positive? Answering these questions will guide you in what you need to do to hold hope high at all costs.

Employee Morale Is Partly Based on Hope

People will persevere and struggle against all odds if they have hope. High employee morale and expectations are based in part on a vision of hope—the hope for greater achievement and success in all areas of life, the hope for a better tomorrow. When you can get your employees to imagine a better way of doing business and then get them to start believing in the power of hope, all kinds of possibilities open up within the organization, giving way to soaring morale.

When managers maintain hope, they also sustain their orga-

Continental Raises Employees' Hopes After Disaster

Airline employees suffered great losses after the September 11 attacks and furloughs for many became inevitable. To build employee hope following the furlough of 4,000 employees, Continental Airlines offered its employees several options: severance payments, the opportunity to transfer to another city or position, and the "promise" of a job when things got better. Continental's actions sent a brave message of hope and trust that its employees would not be forgotten in the wake of the tragedy.

nization's vision. And this can have a dramatic impact and influence on the organization's eventual success.

Take Bill Gates as an example. When he founded Microsoft in 1975, he had a hope and a vision—"a computer on every desk and in every home." He started as a college dropout working in his garage and has revolutionized the way people all over the globe live and do business. Is hope powerful? You bet.

Great managers are dreamers. And when they have hope, that hope inspires those dreams as well as the people who will help make them a reality.

Here's an example. Jeff Bezos, founder and CEO of Amazon.com, has certainly taken the roller coaster ride of Wall Street on more than one occasion, but through it all he's never relinquished his greatest hope and dream for Amazon—from being a successful online bookstore that changed the economics of the book industry to becoming the most phenomenal cyberstore with the world's largest selection of books, videos, music, and more. This is what's called "hope in motion," based on a dream that continues to evolve.

What Is Hope?

Smart Managing What is hope? How do you define it? The following quote might help to guide you:

"Hope begins in the dark, the stubborn hope that if you just show up and try to do the right thing, the dawn will come. You wait and watch and work: you don't give up."

—Anne Lamott, *Bird by Bird*

For Hope to Prevail, Passion Must Endure

There's really only one inherent trait necessary when it comes to holding hope high—especially when times are tough and morale is low—and that's *passion for the people*, the kind of passion that instills in people a belief in the possibilities that lie ahead.

How do you feel about the people on your team? Passionate? How do you feel about what your team is doing? Passionate? Do you believe in the possibilities that lie ahead?

The best managers feel passionate about their work and their employees—and the feeling spreads and inspires.

Managers Are the Guardians of Trust

Trust is essential when it comes to managing others and promoting high performance. In fact, trust is the very foundation upon which all of our relationships are built. Tom Peters may have put it best when he said, "Technique and technology are important, but adding trust is the issue of the decade."

Trust should be treated as a primary management concern. Managers and their employees can perform at their peak only when trust is alive and well within the organization.

Manager's Key Questions on Trust

By answering the following questions, you will gain a greater appreciation for the sanctity of trust and the enormous impact it can have on morale.

- Think of a time when trust in the organization was lost. What was the situation? What were the consequences? How did it make people feel? How did it make you feel?
- Was the lost trust ever regained? If not, why not? If yes, how?
- What do you think is the powerful connection between trust and hope when it comes to building high morale in the workplace?

Trust between managers and employees is something that is earned over time. When a manager breaks a bond of trust with an employee, it is almost impossible to regain or repair.

eBay Builds Success on a Culture of Trust

More than 42 million registered users from all corners of the world participate in online buying, selling, and trading on eBay, the world's most successful Internet company and largest online marketplace. This new form of commerce is built on two pillars: cyberspace capitalism and trust in the basic goodness of people. Intentional or not, eBay has become a testing ground for the debate on the kindness of strangers and trust among one another in our global communities.

So is this organization incredibly naïve and out of touch with reality in today's world or smart to trust that people will do the right thing when given the opportunity? All signs point to the latter.

At eBay, managers have successfully built a worldwide culture of trust. With millions of customers who hardly know one another, the eBay community transacts more than $5 billion in annualized gross merchandise sales (value of goods traded on their site), trusting that every customer will send the money or ship the items as promised.

eBay is banking on the belief that people are basically good—and that trust has been richly rewarded. In the majority of transactions, customers treat each other properly and sometimes even develop friendships. The overwhelmingly positive

TOOLS   **Community Values at eBay**
There are five basic principles by which eBay operates, principles that inspire trust among employees as well as among customers around the world:

We believe people are basically good.
• We believe everyone has something to contribute.
• We believe that an honest, open environment can bring out the best in people.
• We recognize and respect everyone as a unique individual.
• We encourage you to treat others the way you want to be treated.

If you posted these five principles around your workplace, how would people react?

experience seems solid evidence that eBay's culture of trust and faith in people makes good business sense.

Tell Your Employees They're Trustworthy—and Mean It

By trusting your employees, you'll be sending them a strong message that says, "I believe in you and I respect you." Further, it suggests that you have faith in their abilities and competencies and that you believe they've got what it takes to do the job successfully and that they'll do the right thing just because it's the right thing to do.

According to Warren Bennis, trust is the emotional glue that binds followers and leaders together. One way to maintain that bond is to subscribe to, practice, and share with other managers and supervisors the Manager's 12 Tenets of Hope and Trust.

When you are passionate about your hopes and dreams, talk about them. Be yourself, be down-to-earth, and be humble. Your employees will greatly respect your authenticity and your human side.

Manager's 12 Tenets of Hope and Trust

1. Show your respect. This means forget about job titles. Recognize the individual qualities of the people. By showing your respect for others, you and your team will share a stake in the future of the organization and its success.
2. Think before you speak. Be aware not only of *what* you say, but also *how* you say it. Pay attention to your body language, voice inflection, and tone. Often, these things send the loudest message and make the greatest impact.
3. Don't break promises—ever! Do what you say you're going to do. It's as simple as that—and often the secret to a manager's success.
4. Wear one face, not two. You'll lose credibility in a hurry if you tell one person one thing and then someone else somthing different. Management isn't a popularity contest. You'll gain greater trust from people if you are honest and say what you really mean, even if it's not what people want to hear.
5. Let go. That means giving away your power and total responsibility for achieving something of great significance. When you do this,

you give your employees the opportunity to accomplish something great in their own way and you'll be sending a powerful message that says trust, hope, and empowerment are your mantra.

6. Never make a point at someone else's expense. Even when you're kidding, jabs and putdowns are dangerous and can destroy trust in a hurry. Be sensitive to the feelings of others at all times.

7. Dig for the gold in every person and reward the positive. Look for people doing things right and then reward them with praise on the spot. Point out the positives and brag about them.

8. Value other perspectives and views. Remember that everyone operates from a unique map of the world—even you. That perspective is the sum total of life experiences up to that point. Show your appreciation for other people's viewpoints, even when you don't agree. Embrace different opinions and consider each an opportunity from which to learn and grow.

9. Acknowledge that hope and trust flow both ways. Don't expect your employees to have hope if you don't. Don't expect them to have trust in you if you don't trust in them.

10. Keep the faith: have faith in yourself and your people. Show that you believe in your employees. Exhibit confidence and faith in your leadership. No one wants a manager who is tentative.

11. Believe in the possibilities and keep hope alive at all costs. Paint a picture of unlimited possibilities for your employees and let them know that you believe in their potential and that their talents and interests are worth developing.

12. Be authentic—act human. So what if you're the manager? You're human too! When you blow it, 'fess up. Never cover up your mistakes or you will lose all credibility.

Managers Must Keep the Faith

The basic definition of "faith" is confidence or trust in a person or thing. So, "keeping the faith" means holding to something more meaningful than the bottom line, whatever that might be to the individual, and tapping into the power of that faith when it's needed most.

Smart managers have faith in the power of love and respect for their people, both as employees and as fellow humans. It's imperative that managers use faith as a meaningful way to build fast-moving, competitive companies with consistently high employee morale.

The Importance of Faith

We all know people who lack faith. They may lack faith in themselves, their leaders, their families and friends, or their jobs. Their lack of faith undermines their ability to perform at their best and maintain positive work morale. Work becomes just a paycheck. When employees lose faith, managers lose the best that they can get from their people.

Men and women everywhere are seeking something that they can believe in and hold on to in their lives in general and in their jobs. More than ever before, employees want and need better reasons to go to work each day. There are deep inner needs, more than ever before, that they're trying to fill. Managers have the daunting task of finding creative ways to help them fill their needs whenever possible.

So, what do employees want to have faith in? For starters, they want to have faith in knowing that their ideas and suggestions are good. They want to believe and have faith that the time they spend at work is worth it and part of something greater. They want to have faith in their managers and know that they can trust their word. They also want to have faith in the products and services they provide and the customers who buy those products and services.

But there's an even larger issue at stake here—passion. Because when people lose their faith, they often lose their passion and drive along with it. And that can sap employee morale and motivation.

Faith in ourselves lights the flame within that ultimately sustains us through the toughest of times, renews our vitality and energy when we need them most, and makes us more powerful, self-assured, and at peace with our direction. This is why it is important for managers to encourage and build faith among their employees. Faith strengthens us by feeding passion to the brain as well as to the heart.

Managers Must Believe in a Better Tomorrow

We build morale partly on the foundation of our belief in a better tomorrow—the hope for a brighter, more rewarding future for ourselves and our children. Today, employees still want to know what life could be and they look to their leaders to move them toward that answer and provide hope and inspiration.

When people believe in the possibilities, guess what? Things get better. Poof! It's automatic.

A great example of this can be seen in the uplifting movie *Phenomenon* (1996), the story of an ordinary man transformed by extraordinary events. The man is George Malley (played by John Travolta). In the beginning of the movie, George is knocked to the ground by a mysterious and blinding light. From that moment, George shows amazing abilities: he can read and understand volumes of books at record speed, he develops instant fluency in other languages, and he learns the intricacies of science and medicine without difficulty.

His prodigious abilities affect people from miles around and boost the morale of the small community. Everyone, including George, assumes that his extraordinary talents are surely the result of some supernatural power or perhaps a spell placed on him from outer space. Later when it's revealed that George has a terminal brain tumor that caused the bright flash of light that changed his life, he makes a profound discovery.

George experiences an epiphany when he discovers that it was he all along who performed the amazing feats. He simply learned to maximize his natural potential.

Although it might be tempting to dismiss this movie as just a piece of fiction, it should make us wonder about the potential that lies within each of us. It should also make you as a manager think about the potential in your employees and how to help them develop it.

It's your responsibility to hold hope, trust, and faith high for your employees—to help create small and large epiphanies of what life could be. That's the spirit, that's the challenge. Are you ready for the expedition?

Smart Managers—Sources of Hope, Trust, and Faith

There are a variety of ways that managers and their organizations can successfully proclaim hope, trust, and faith in their people and their organizations. Some of those actions may look like wise management decisions: supporting minority businesses, investing in healthcare benefits for both full- and part-time workers, or simply promoting from within. No matter how you choose to convey your belief in a brighter tomorrow, the result will be that most employees will become more empowered and alive with possibilities.

Top Companies That Promote High Morale with Hope, Trust, Faith, and Belief

We'll close this chapter on engendering hope, trust, faith, and belief in a better tomorrow with a few examples of companies that are doing just that.

Marriott International: At Marriott the possibilities are endless. Hourly associates can make it to the top as senior vice presidents. And why not? There's lots of coaching in the hotel chain, continuous educational programs, and off-site conferences to attend.

Schering-Plough: This drug company helps minority students learn to be lab technicians and in the process learn more about the business and about opportunities open to them in the health sciences professions.

Starbucks: It doesn't matter if you're a part-timer here. Part-timers are valued highly and enjoy the perks of full-time benefits, like medical, dental, and vision coverage.

McDonald's: In an effort to support minority-owned businesses, the hamburger king spends $3 billion a year (more than 27% of its total) with minority-owned companies, such as bakeries that supply the fast-food chain with buns.

TIAA-CREF: This top pension firm grooms minorities for executive positions by rotating workers through different departments—including the chairman's office! Talk about building high employee morale!

Johnson & Johnson: Committed to providing a better tomorrow for its employees' children, the widely respected healthcare company operates six centers that care for 1,400 children of Johnson & Johnson employees.

Pfizer: The popular pharmaceutical company knows that one way to employees' hearts is through their stomachs. The company provides a subsidized cafeteria for all workers, which also allows them to order a take-home dinner for the family and have it delivered to their offices by the end of the day.

Harley-Davidson: Employees who fantasize about riding their own "hog" on the open road can make the dream a reality with the company's "Easy Own" program that assists employees in getting their own Harley in no time. Here's how the three-year special financing package works. Year one, employees pay zero—that's right, no interest, no payments. Year two, employees make payments only on the principal owed, but pay no interest. Year three, employees start making regular payments and can extend financing if necessary. Born to be wild? Yep! Born to be generous too.

Texas Instruments: Employees who need a college degree to broaden their horizons just ask their manager and TI will pay for tuition, fees, and books.

Start thinking about new ways you too can positively affect the environment and the morale of your employees by coming up with your own unique approaches for showing your commitment to a brighter future for everyone.

Manager's Checklist for Chapter 10

❏ Hope can be a manager's greatest weapon when fighting low employee morale.

❏ Employee morale is based partly on vision and hope for a better tomorrow.

❑ Trust is the issue of the decade and should be treated as a primary management concern.

❑ Trust is something that must be earned over time.

❑ Employees need to have faith that the time they spend at work promotes a greater cause and mission.

❑ Employees need to have faith in their leaders and know that they can trust their word.

❑ When people believe in the possibilities, the future becomes brighter.

❑ Managers should help create epiphanies, large and small, for their workers of what life could be.

Index